P. Schalow
Dec. 4, 2012

German

phrase book & dictionary

Richard-Wagner-Platz

Berlitz Publishing
New York London Singapore

Contacting the Editors
Every effort has been made to provide accurate information in this publication, but changes are inevitable. The publisher cannot be responsible for any resulting loss, inconvenience or injury. We would appreciate it if readers would call our attention to any errors or outdated information. We also welcome your suggestions; if you come across a relevant expression not in our phrase book, please contact us at: **comments@berlitzpublishing.com**

All Rights Reserved
© 2007 Berlitz Publishing/APA Publications (UK) Ltd.
Berlitz Trademark Reg. U.S. Patent Office and other countries. Marca Registrada. Used under license from Berlitz Investment Corporation.

Eleventh Printing: March 2012
Printed in China

Publishing Director: Mina Patria
Commissioning Editor: Kate Drynan
Editorial Assistant: Sophie Cooper
Translation: updated by Wordbank
Cover Design: Beverley Speight
Interior Design: Beverley Speight
Production Manager: Raj Trivedi
Picture Researcher: Lucy Johnston
Cover Photo: Jon Santa-Cruz/APA except Bauhaus shot Glyn Genin/APA
Currency shot: Lucy Johnston/APA

Interior Photos: Kevin Cummins 51; Glyn Genin/APA 68, 72, 82, 85, 88, 118; Greg Gladman/APA 134; iStockphoto 14, 58, 129, 133, 144, 146, 149, 156, 168; Britta Jaschinski/APA 39, 97, 102; Lucy Johnston/APA 17, 172; Jon Santa-Cruz/APA 12, 28, 60, 71, 74, 79, 94, 104, 108, 111, 117, 123, 136, 139, 140, 143; Slovenia info 127, 130

Contents

Pronunciation	7	Vowels	9
Consonants	7	How to use this Book	10

Survival

Arrival & Departure	**13**	Parking	36
ESSENTIAL	13	Breakdown & Repair	37
Border Control	14	Accidents	37
Money	**15**	**Places to Stay**	**37**
ESSENTIAL	15	ESSENTIAL	37
At the Bank	16	Somewhere to Stay	38
		At the Hotel	39
Getting Around	**18**	Price	41
ESSENTIAL	18	Preferences	42
Tickets	19	Questions	42
Plane	20	Problems	43
Airport Transfer	20	Checking Out	44
Checking In	22	Renting	45
Luggage	22	Domestic Items	46
Finding your Way	24	At the Hostel	47
Train	24	Going Camping	48
Departures	26		
On Board	26	**Communications**	**49**
Bus	27	ESSENTIAL	49
U-Bahn	28	Online	50
Boat & Ferry	29	Social Media	51
Taxi	30	Phone	53
Bicycle & Motorbike	32	Telephone Etiquette	56
Car Hire	32	Fax	56
Fuel Station	33	Post	57
Asking Directions	34		

Food & Drink

Eating Out 59
ESSENTIAL 59
Where to Eat 60
Reservations & Preferences 61
How to Order 62
Cooking Methods 63
Dietary Requirements 64
Dining with Children 65
How to Complain 65
Paying 66

Meals & Cooking 67
Breakfast 67
Appetizers 68
Soup 69
Fish & Seafood 70
Meat & Poultry 71

Vegetables & Staples 73
Fruit 74
Cheese 75
Dessert 75
Sauces & Condiments 76
At the Market 76
In the Kitchen 77

Drinks 79
ESSENTIAL 79
Non-alcoholic Drinks 80
Aperitifs, Cocktails & Liqueurs 81
Beer 82
Wine 83

On the Menu 83

People

Conversation 95
ESSENTIAL 95
Language Difficulties 96
Making Friends 97
Travel Talk 98
Personal 98
Work & School 99

Weather 100
Romance 101
ESSENTIAL 101
The Dating Game 101
Accepting & Rejecting 102
Getting Intimate 103
Sexual Preferences 103

Leisure Time

Sightseeing	**105**	Fabric	120
ESSENTIAL	105	Shoes	121
Tourist Information	105	Sizes	121
On Tour	105	Newsagent & Tobacconist	121
Seeing the Sights	107	Photography	122
Religious Sites	108	Souvenirs	123
Shopping	**109**	**Sport & Leisure**	**125**
ESSENTIAL	109	ESSENTIAL	125
At the Shops	109	Watching Sport	125
Ask an Assistant	110	Playing Sport	126
Personal Preferences	112	At the Beach/Pool	127
Paying & Bargaining	113	Winter Sports	129
Making a Complaint	114	Out in the Country	131
Services	115		
Hair & Beauty	115	**Going Out**	**132**
Antiques	117	ESSENTIAL	132
Clothing	117	Entertainment	133
Colors	118	Nightlife	134
Clothes & Accessories	119		

Special Requirements

Business Travel	**137**	Baby Essentials	142
ESSENTIAL	137	Babysitting	142
On Business	137	Health & Emergency	143
Traveling with Children	**140**	**Disabled Travelers**	**144**
ESSENTIAL	140	ESSENTIAL	144
Out & About	141	Asking for Assistance	145

6

In an Emergency

Emergencies	**147**	Basic Supplies	158
ESSENTIAL	147		
		The Basics	**159**
Police	**148**	Grammar	159
ESSENTIAL	148	Numbers	165
Crime & Lost Property	148	ESSENTIAL	165
		Ordinal Numbers	166
Health	**150**	Time	166
ESSENTIAL	150	ESSENTIAL	166
Finding a Doctor	150	Days	167
Symptoms	151	ESSENTIAL	167
Conditions	152	Dates	168
Treatment	153	Months	168
Hospital	153	Seasons	169
Dentist	154	Holidays	169
Gynecologist	154	Conversion Tables	170
Optician	155	Kilometers to Miles Conversions	171
Payment & Insurance	155	Measurement	171
Pharmacy	155	Temperature	171
ESSENTIAL	155	Oven Temperature	171
What to Take	156		

Dictionary

English-German Dictionary	173	German-English Dictionary	199

Pronunciation

This section is designed to make you familiar with the sounds of German, using our simplified phonetic transcription. You'll find the pronunciation of the German letters explained below, together with their 'imitated' equivalents. This system is used throughout the phrase book; simply read the pronunciation as if it were English, noting any special rules below.

The German alphabet is the same as English, with the addition of the letter **ß**. Some vowels appear with an **Umlaut: ä, ü** and **ö**. Of note, German recently underwent a spelling reform. The letter **ß** is now shown as **ss** after a short vowel, but is unchanged after a long vowel or diphthong. In print and dated material, you may still see the **ß**; e.g., formerly **Kuß**, now **Kuss**.

Stress has been indicated in the phonetic transcription: the underlined letters should be pronounced with more stress, e.g., *Adresse, ah-drehs-uh*.

Consonants

Letter	Approximate Pronunciation	Symbol	Example	Pronunciation
b	1. at the end of a word or between a vowel and a consonant, like p in up	p	**ab**	*ahp*
	2. elsewhere, as in English	b	**bis**	*bihs*
c	1. before e, i, ä and ö, like ts in hits	ts	**Celsius**	*tsehl•see•oos*
	2. elsewhere, like c in cat	k	**Café**	*kah•feh*
ch	1. like k in kit	k	**Wachs**	*vahks*
	2. after vowels, like ch in Scottish loch	kh	**doch**	*dohkh*

Letter	Approximate Pronunciation	Symbol	Example	Pronunciation
d	1. at the end of the word or before a consonant, like t in eat	t	**Rad**	*raht*
	2. elsewhere, like d in do	d	**danke**	*dahn•kuh*
g	1. at the end of a word, sounds like k	k	**fertig**	*fehr•teek*
	2. like g in go	g	**gehen**	*geh•uhn*
j	like y in yes	y	**ja**	*yah*
qu	like k + v	kv	**Quark**	*kvahrk*
r	pronounced in the back of the mouth	r	**warum**	*vah•room*
s	1. before or between vowels, like z in zoo	z	**sie**	*zee*
	2. before p and t, like sh in shut	sh	**Sport**	*shpohrt*
	3. elsewhere, like s in sit	s	**es ist**	*ehs ihst*
ß	like s in sit	s	**groß**	*grohs*
sch	like sh in shut	sh	**schnell**	*shnehl*
tsch	like ch in chip	ch	**deutsch**	*doych*
tz	like ts in hits	ts	**Platz**	*plahts*
v	1. like f in for	f	**vier**	*feer*
	2. in foreign words, like v in voice	v	**Vase**	*vah•seh*
w	like v in voice	v	**wie**	*vee*
z	like ts in hits	ts	**zeigen**	*tsie•gehn*

Letters f, h, k, l, m, n, p, t and x are pronounced as in English.

Vowels

Letter	Approximate Pronunciation	Symbol	Example	Pronunciation
a	like a in father	**ah**	**Tag**	*tahk*
ä	1. like e in let	**eh**	**Lärm**	*lehrm*
	2. like a in late	**ay**	**spät**	*shpayt*
e	1. like e in let	**eh**	**schnell**	*shnehl*
	2. at the end of a word, if the syllable is not stressed, like u in us	**uh**	**bitte**	*biht•tuh*
i	1. like i in hit, before a doubled consonant	**ih**	**billig**	*bih•leek*
	2. otherwise, like ee in meet	**ee**	**ihm**	*eem*
o	like o in home	**oh**	**voll**	*fohl*
ö	like er in fern	**er**	**schön**	*shern*
u	like oo in boot	**oo**	**Nuss**	*noos*
ü	like ew in new	**ew**	**über**	*ew•behr*
y	like ew in new	**ew**	**typisch**	*tew•peesh*

Combined Vowels

Letter	Approximate Pronunciation	Symbol	Example	Pronunciation
ai, ay, ei, ey	like ie in tie	**ie**	**nein**	*nien*
ao, au	like ow in now	**ow**	**auf**	*owf*
äu, eu, oy	like oy in boy oy	**oy**	**neu**	*noy*

How to use this Book

> Sometimes you see two alternatives separated by a slash. Choose the one that's right for your situation.

ESSENTIAL

When does the bank open/close?

Wann öffnet/schließt die Bank? *vahn erf•nuht/ shleest dee bahnk*

I'd like to change dollars/pounds into euros.

Ich möchte Dollar/Pfund in Euro wechseln. *eekh mehrkh•tuh doh•lahr/pfoont ihn oy•roh vehkh•zuhln*

I'd like to cash traveler's checks [cheques].

Ich möchte Reiseschecks einlösen. *eekh mehrkh•tuh rie•zuh•shehks ien•ler•zuhn*

> Words you may see are shown in YOU MAY SEE boxes.

YOU MAY SEE...

ZOLL	customs
ZOLLFREIE WAREN	duty-free goods
ZOLLPFLICHTIGE WAREN	goods to declare

> Any of the words or phrases listed can be plugged into the sentence below.

Tickets

When's...to Berlin?

Wann geht . . . nach Berlin? *vahn geht . . . nahkh behr•leen*

the (first) bus

der (erste) Bus *dehr (ehr•stuh) boos*

the (next) flight

der (nächste) Flug *dehr (nehks•tuh) floog*

the (last) train

der (letzte) Zug *dehr (lehts•tuh) tsoog*

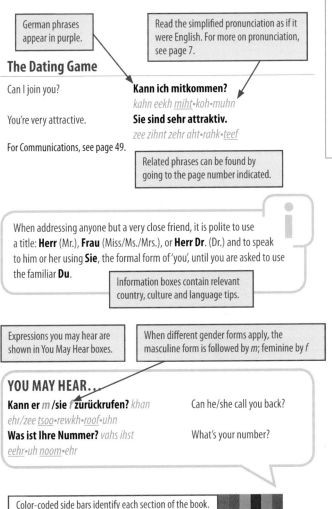

German phrases appear in purple.

Read the simplified pronunciation as if it were English. For more on pronunciation, see page 7.

The Dating Game

Can I join you?

Kann ich mitkommen?
kahn eekh miht·koh·muhn

You're very attractive.

Sie sind sehr attraktiv.
zee zihnt zehr aht·rahk·teef

For Communications, see page 49.

Related phrases can be found by going to the page number indicated.

When addressing anyone but a very close friend, it is polite to use a title: **Herr** (Mr.), **Frau** (Miss/Ms./Mrs.), or **Herr Dr**. (Dr.) and to speak to him or her using **Sie**, the formal form of 'you', until you are asked to use the familiar **Du**.

Information boxes contain relevant country, culture and language tips.

Expressions you may hear are shown in You May Hear boxes.

When different gender forms apply, the masculine form is followed by *m*; feminine by *f*

YOU MAY HEAR...

Kann er *m*/sie *f* zurückrufen? *khan ehr/zee tsoo·rewkh·roof·uhn*

Can he/she call you back?

Was ist Ihre Nummer? *vahs ihst eehr·uh noom·ehr*

What's your number?

Color-coded side bars identify each section of the book.

Survival

Arrival & Departure   13
Money   15
Getting Around   18
Places to Stay   37
Communications   49

ESSENTIAL

I'm on vacation [holiday].	**Ich mache Urlaub.** *eekh mahkh•uh oor•lowb*
I'm on business.	**Ich bin auf Geschäftsreise.** *eekh bihn owf guh•shehfts•rie•zuh*
I'm going to...	**Ich reise nach ...** *eekh rie•zuh nahkh ...*
I'm staying at the...Hotel.	**Ich übernachte im Hotel ...** *eekh ew•buhr•nahkh•tuh ihm hoh•tehl ...*

YOU MAY HEAR...

Ihren Reisepass, bitte. *eer•uhn rie•zuh•pahs biht•tuh*
Your passport, please.

Was ist der Grund Ihrer Reise? *vahs ihst dehr groont ihr•uhr rie•zuh*
What's the purpose of your visit?

Wo übernachten Sie? *voh ew•behr•nahkh•tuhn zee*
Where are you staying?

Wie lange bleiben Sie? *vee lahng•uh blie•buhn zee*
How long are you staying?

Mit wem reisen Sie? *miht vehm rie•zuhn zee*
Who are you traveling with?

Border Control

I'm just passing through.	**Ich bin auf der Durchreise.** *eekh been owf dehr <u>doorkh</u>•rie•zuh*
I'd like to declare…	**Ich möchte … verzollen.** *eekh <u>merkh</u>•tuh … fehr•<u>tsoh</u>•luhn*
I have nothing to declare.	**Ich habe nichts zu verzollen.** *eekh <u>hah</u>•buh neekhts tsoo fehr•<u>tsoh</u>•luhn*

YOU MAY HEAR…

Haben Sie etwas zu verzollen? *<u>hah</u>•buhn zee <u>eht</u>•vahs tsoo fehr•<u>tsoh</u>•luhn*
Do you have anything to declare?

Darauf müssen Sie Zoll zahlen. *dahr•<u>owf</u> <u>mew</u>•suhn zee tsol <u>tsah</u>•luhn*
You must pay duty on this.

Öffnen Sie diese Tasche. *<u>erf</u>•nuhn zee <u>dee</u>•zuh <u>tah</u>•shuh*
Open this bag.

YOU MAY SEE...

ZOLL	customs
ZOLLFREIE WAREN	duty-free goods
ZOLLPFLICHTIGE WAREN	goods to declare
NICHTS ZU VERZOLLEN	nothing to declare
PASSKONTROLLE	passport control
POLIZEI	police

Money

ESSENTIAL

Where's...?	**Wo ist ...?** *voh ihst ...*
the ATM	**der Bankautomat** *dehr <u>bahnk</u>•ow•toh•maht*
the bank	**die Bank** *dee bahnk*
the currency exchange office	**die Wechselstube** *dee <u>vehkh</u>•zuhl•shtoo•buh*
When does the bank open/close?	**Wann öffnet/schließt die Bank?** *vahn <u>erf</u>•nuht/ shleest dee bahnk*
I'd like to change dollars/pounds into euros.	**Ich möchte Dollar/Pfund in Euro wechseln.** *eekh <u>mehrkh</u>•tuh <u>doh</u>•lahr/pfoont ihn <u>oy</u>•roh <u>vehkh</u>•zuhln*
I'd like to cash traveler's checks [cheques].	**Ich möchte Reiseschecks einlösen.** *eekh <u>mehrkh</u>•tuh <u>rie</u>•zuh•shehks ien•<u>ler</u>•zuhn*

At the Bank

I'd like to change money/get a cash advance.	**Ich möchte Geld wechseln.** *eekh mehrkh•tuh gehlt vehkh•zuhln*
What's the exchange rate/fee?	**Was ist der Wechselkurs/die Gebühr?** *vahs ihst dehr vehkh•zuhl•koors/dee guh•bewr*
I think there's a mistake.	**Ich glaube, hier stimmt etwas nicht.** *eekh glow•buh heer shtihmt eht•vahs neekht*
I lost my traveler's cheques.	**Ich habe meine Reiseschecks verloren.** *eekh hah•buh mie•nuh rie•zuh•shecks fehr•loh•ruhn*
My card was stolen/doesn't work.	**Meine Karte wurde gestohlen/funktioniert nicht.** *mie•nuh kahr•tuh voor•duh guh•shtoh•luhn/ foonk•tzyoh•neert neekht*
My card was lost.	**Ich habe meine Karte verloren.** *eek hah•buh mie•nuh kahr•tuh fehr•loh•ruhn*
The ATM ate my card.	**Der Bankautomat hat meine Karte eingezogen.** *dehr bahnk•ow•toh•maht haht mie•nuh kahr•tuh ien•geh•tsoh•ghun*

YOU MAY SEE...

KARTE HIER EINFÜHREN	insert card here
ABBRECHEN	cancel
LÖSCHEN	clear
EINGEBEN	enter
PIN-NUMMER	PIN
ABHEBUNG	withdrawal
VOM GIROKONTO	from checking [current] account
VOM SPARKONTO	from savings account
QUITTUNG	receipt

The best rates for exchanging money will be found at banks.
You can also change money at travel agencies, currency exchange
offices and hotels, though the rate may not be as good. Traveler's
checks are accepted at most banks (though banks are not required to
accept them) and currency exchange offices, but a variable fee will be
charged. Cash can be obtained from **Bankautomaten** (ATMs) with
many international bank and credit cards. ATMs are multilingual, so
English-language instructions can be selected. Remember to bring your
passport when you want to change money.

For Numbers, see page 165.

YOU MAY SEE...

German currency is the **Euro €**, divided into 100 **Cent**.
Coins: 1, 2, 5, 10, 20, 50 **Cent**; €1, 2
Notes: €5, 10, 20, 50, 100, 200, 500

Getting Around

ESSENTIAL

How do I get to town?	**Wie komme ich in die Stadt?**
	vee koh·muh eekh ihn dee shtaht
Where's …?	**Wo ist …?** *voh ihst …*
the airport	**der Flughafen** *dehr flook·hah·fuhn*
the train [railway] station	**der Bahnhof** *dehr bahn·hohf*
the bus station	**die Bushaltestelle** *dee boos·hahl·tuh·shteh·luh*
the subway [underground] station	**die U-Bahn-Haltestelle** *dee oo·bahn·hahl·tuh·shteh·luh*
Is it far from here?	**Wie weit ist es?** *vee viet ihst ehs*
Where do I buy a ticket?	**Wo kann ich eine Fahrkarte kaufen?** *voh kahn eekh ie·nuh fahr·kahr·tuh kow·fuhn*
A one-way/return ticket to…	**Ein Einzelticket/Eine Fahrkarte für Hin- und Rückfahrt nach …** *ien ien·tsehl·tee·kuht/ie·nuh fahr·kahr·tuh fewr hihn oond rewk·fahrt nahkh…*
How much?	**Wie viel kostet es?** *vee feel kohs·tuht ehs*
Which gate/line?	**Welches Gate/Linie?** *vehl·khehs geht/leen·yah*
Which platform?	**Welcher Bahnsteig?** *vehl·khehr bahn·shtieg*
Where can I get a taxi?	**Wo finde ich ein Taxi?** *voh fihn·duh eekh ien tahk·see*
Take me to this address, please.	**Bitte fahren Sie mich zu dieser Adresse.** *biht·tuh fah·ruhn zee meekh tsoo dee·zehr ah·dreh·suh*
Can I have a map, please?	**Können Sie mir bitte einen Stadtplan geben?** *ker·nuhn zee mihr biht·tuh ien·uhn shtaht·plahn geh·behn*

Tickets

When's…to Berlin?	**Wann geht … nach Berlin?** *vahn geht … nahkh behr-leen*
the (first) bus	**der (erste) Bus** *dehr (ehr-stuh) boos*
the (next) flight	**der (nächste) Flug** *dehr (nehks-tuh) floog*
the (last) train	**der (letzte) Zug** *dehr (lehts-tuh) tsoog*
Where do I buy…?	**Wo kaufe ich …?** *voh kow-fuh eekh …*
One/two airline ticket(s), please.	**Ein/Zwei Ticket(s), bitte.** *ien/tsvie tee-kuht(s) biht-tuh*
One/two (bus/train/subway) ticket(s), please.	**Ein/Zwei Fahrkarte(n), bitte.** *ien/tsvie fahr-kahr-tuh(n) biht-tuh*
For today/tomorrow.	**Für heute/morgen.** *fewr hoy-tuh/mohr-guhn*
A…(airline) ticket.	**Ein … Ticket.** *ien … tee-kuht*
one-way	**einfaches** *ien-fah-khuhs*
return trip	**Hin- und Rückflug-** *hihn oont rewk-floog*
first class	**Erste-Klasse-** *ehr-stuh-klah-suh*
business class	**Business-Class-** *bihz-nehs-klahs*
economy class	**Economy-Class-** *eh-koh-noh-mee-klahs*
A…(bus/train/subway) ticket.	**Eine … ** *ie-nuh …*
one-way	**Einzelfahrkarte** *ien-zuhl-fahr-karh-tuh*
return trip	**Hin- und Rückfahrkarte** *hihn oont rewk-fahr-kahr-tuh*
first class	**Erste-Klasse-Fahrkarte** *ehr-stuh-klah-suh-fahr-karh-tuh*
How much?	**Wie viel kostet es?** *vee feel kohs-tuht ehs*
Can I buy a ticket on the bus/train?	**Kann ich im Bus/Zug eine Fahrkarte kaufen?** *kahn eekh ihm boos/tsoog ie-nuh fahr-kahr-tuh kow-fuhn*
I have an airline/a train e-ticket.	**Ich habe ein E-Ticket/Online-Ticket.** *eekh hah-buh ien ay-tee-keht/ohn-lien-tee-keht*

Is there a discount for...?	**Gibt es eine Ermäßigung für ...?** *gihpt ehs ie•nuh ehr•meh•see•goong fewr ...*
children	**Kinder** *kihn•dehr*
students	**Studenten** *shtoo•deh•tuhn*
senior citizens	**Rentner** *rehnt•nehr*
tourists	**Touristen** *too•rih•stuhn*
The express/local bus/train, please.	**Den Express-/Nahverkehrs-Bus/Zug, bitte.** *dehn ehks•prehs•/nah•fuhr•kehrs•boos/tsoog biht•tuh*
Do I have to stamp the ticket before boarding?	**Muss ich das Ticket vor dem Einsteigen entwerten?** *Moos eekh dahs tihk•khet fohr dehm ayn•shtayg•uhn ehnt•vehr•thun*
How long is this ticket valid?	**Wie lange ist das Ticket gültig?** *vee lahng•uh ihst dahs tihk•khet gewl•teekh*
Can I return on the same ticket?	**Kann ich mit demselben Ticket zurückfahren?** *kahn eekh miht dehm•sehl•bhun tihk•khet tsoo•rewkh•fah•ruhn*
I'd like to... my reservation.	**Ich möchte meine Reservierung ...** *eekh merkh•tuh mie•nuh reh•zehr•vee•roong ...*
cancel	**stornieren** *shtohr•nee•ruhn*
change	**ändern** *ehn•dehrn*
confirm	**bestätigen** *beh•shtay•tee•guhn*

For Days, see page 167.
For Time, see page 166.

Plane

Airport Transfer

| How much is a taxi to the airport? | **Was kostet ein Taxi zum Flughafen?** *vahs kohs•tuht ien tahk•see tsoom flook•hah•fuhn* |
| To...Airport, please. | **Zum Flughafen ..., bitte.** *tsoom flook•hah•fuhn ... biht•tuh* |

My airline is...	**Meine Fluggesellschaft ist ...**
	mie•nuh floo•geh•zehl•shahft ihst ...
My flight leaves at...	**Mein Flug geht um ...** _mien floog geht oom ..._
I'm in a rush.	**Ich habe es eilig.** _eekh hah•buh ehs ie•leek_
Can you take an alternate route?	**Können Sie eine andere Strecke fahren?**
	ker•nuhn zee ie•nuh ahn•deh•ruh shtreh•kuh fah•ruhn
Can you drive faster/slower?	**Können Sie schneller/langsamer fahren?**
	ker•nuhn zee shneh•lehr/lahng•sah•mehr fah•ruhn

YOU MAY HEAR...

Mit welcher Fluggesellschaft fliegen Sie?	Which airline are you flying?
meet vehlkh•ehr floog•geh•sehl•shahft flee•gehn zee	
Inland oder international? _ihn•lahnt oh•dehr ihn•tuhr•nah•syoh•nahl_	Domestic or international?
Welcher Terminal? _vehlkh•ehr tehr•mee•nahl_	What terminal?

YOU MAY SEE...

ANKUNFT	arrivals
ABFLUG	departures
GEPÄCKAUSGABE	baggage claim
INLANDSFLÜGE	domestic flights
INTERNATIONALE FLÜGE	international flights
CHECK-IN	check-in
E-TICKET CHECK-IN	e-ticket check-in
ABFLUG-GATES	departure gates

Checking In

Where's check-in?	**Wo ist das Check-in?** *voh ihst dahs <u>tshehk</u>·in*
My name is…	**Mein Name ist …** *mien <u>nahm</u>·uh ihst …*
I'm going to…	**Ich reise nach …** *eekh <u>riez</u>·uh nahkh …*
I have…	**Ich habe …** *eekh <u>hahb</u>·uh …*
one suitcase	**einen Koffer** *<u>ien</u>·uhn <u>kohf</u>·fehr*
two suitcases	**zwei Koffer** *tsvie <u>kohf</u>·fehr*
one piece of hand luggage	**ein Handgepäckstück** *ien <u>hahnd</u>·guh·pehk·shtewk*
How much luggage is allowed?	**Wie viel Gepäck ist erlaubt?** *vee feel guh·<u>pehk</u> ihst ehr·<u>lowbt</u>*
Is that pounds or kilos?	**Sind das Pfund oder Kilo?** *zihnt dahs pfoont <u>oh</u>·duhr <u>kee</u>·loh*
Which terminal?	**Welcher Terminal?** *<u>vehlkh</u>·ehr tehr·mee·<u>nahl</u>*
Which gate?	**Welches Gate?** *<u>vehlkh</u>·uhs geht*
I'd like a window/an aisle seat.	**Ich möchte gern einen Fensterplatz/Platz am Gang.** *eekh <u>merkht</u>·uh gehrn <u>ien</u>·uhn <u>fehnst</u>·ehr·plahts/plahts ahm gahng*
When do we leave/arrive?	**Wann ist der Abflug/die Ankunft?** *vahn ihst dehr <u>ahp</u>·floog/dee <u>ahn</u>·kuhnft*
Is the flight delayed?	**Hat der Flug Verspätung?** *haht dehr floog fehr·<u>shpeh</u>·toong*
How late?	**Wie viel?** *vee feel*

Luggage

Where is/are…?	**Wo ist/sind …?** *voh ihst/zihnt …*
the luggage trolleys	**die Gepäckwagen** *dee guh·<u>pehk</u>·vah·guhn*
the luggage lockers	**die Gepäckschließfächer** *dee guh·<u>pehk</u>·shlees·fehkh·ehr*

YOU MAY HEAR...

Der Nächste, bitte! *dehr <u>nehkhst</u>•uh <u>biht</u>•tuh*
Next, please!

Ihren Reisepass/Ihr Ticket, bitte.
eehr•uhn <u>riez</u>•uh•pahs/eehr tih•kuht <u>biht</u>•tuh
Your passport/ticket, please.

Geben Sie Gepäck auf? *<u>gehb</u>•ehn zee guh•<u>pehk</u> owf*
Are you checking in any luggage?

Das ist zu groß für Handgepäck. *dahs ihst tsoo grohs fuehr <u>hahnd</u>•guh•pehk*
That's too large for a carry-on [piece of hand luggage].

Haben Sie diese Taschen selbst gepackt?
<u>hah</u>•buhn zee <u>dees</u>•uh <u>tahsh</u>•uhn sehlbst guh•<u>pahkt</u>
Did you pack these bags yourself?

Hat Ihnen jemand etwas mitgegeben?
haht <u>eehn</u>•uhn <u>yeh</u>•mahnd <u>eht</u>•vahs <u>miht</u>•guh•geh•buhn
Did anyone give you anything to carry?

Leeren Sie Ihre Taschen. *<u>lehr</u>•uhn zee <u>eehr</u>•uh <u>tahsh</u>•uhn*
Empty your pockets.

Ziehen Sie Ihre Schuhe aus. *<u>tsee</u>•uhn zee <u>eehr</u>•uh <u>shoo</u>•uh ows*
Take off your shoes.

Wir beginnen jetzt mit dem Einsteigen ...
weer beh•<u>gihn</u>•nuhn yehtst miht dehm <u>ayn</u>•shtayg•uhn ...
We are now boarding...

the baggage claim **die Gepäckausgabe** *dee guh•<u>pehk</u>•ows•gahb•uh*

My luggage has been lost/stolen. **Mein Gepäck ist weg/wurde gestohlen.** *mien guh•<u>pehk</u> ihst vehk/<u>voor</u>•duh guh•<u>shtohl</u>•uhn*

My suitcase is damaged. **Mein Koffer wurde beschädigt.** *mien <u>kohf</u>•fehr <u>voord</u>•uh buh•<u>shehd</u>•eekht*

Finding your Way

Where is/are ...?	**Wo ist/sind ...?** *voh ihst/zihnt ...*
the currency exchange	**die Wechselstube** *dee vehkh-zuhl-shtoo-buh*
the car hire	**die Autovermietung** *dee ow-toh-fehr-meet-oong*
the exit	**der Ausgang** *dehr ows-gahng*
the taxis	**die Taxis** *dee tahks-ees*
Is there a ... into town?	**Gibt es ... in die Stadt?** *gihbt ehs ... ihn dee shtadt*
bus	**einen Bus** *ien-uhn boos*
train	**einen Zug** *ien-uhn tsoog*
subway [underground]	**eine U-Bahn** *ien-uh oo-bahn*

For Asking Directions, see page 34.

Train

Where's the train [railway] station?	**Wo ist der Bahnhof?** *voh ihst dehr bahn-hohf*
How far is it?	**Wie weit ist es?** *vee viet ihst ehs*
Where is/are ...?	**Wo ist/sind ...?** *voh ihst/zihnt ...*
the ticket office	**der Fahrkartenschalter** *dehr fahr-kahrt-uhn-shahl-tehr*
the information desk	**die Information** *dee ihn-fohrm-ah-syohn*
the luggage lockers	**die Gepäckschließfächer** *dee guh-pehk-shlees-fehkh-ehr*
the platforms	**die Bahnsteige** *dee bahn-shtieg-uh*
Can I have a schedule [timetable]?	**Kann ich einen Fahrplan haben?** *kahn eehk ien-uhn fahr-plahn hah-buhn*
How long is the trip?	**Wie lange dauert die Fahrt?** *vee lahng-uh dow-ehrt dee fahrt*

Is it a direct train?	**Ist das eine direkte Zugverbindung?**
	ihst dahs <u>ien</u>•uh dee•<u>rehkt</u> tsoog•ver•<u>bind</u>•ungh
Do I have to change trains?	**Muss ich umsteigen?** *moos eekh <u>oom</u>•shtieg•uhn*
Is the train on time?	**Ist der Zug pünktlich?** *ihst dehr tsoog <u>pewnkt</u>•leekh*

For Asking Directions, see page 34.

For Tickets, see page 19.

YOU MAY SEE...

BAHNSTEIGE	platforms
INFORMATION	information
RESERVIERUNGEN	reservations
WARTERAUM	waiting room
ANKUNFT	arrivals
ABFAHRT	departures

German trains are fast, comfortable and reliable. Train travel in Germany is a highly recommended alternative to driving. The **Deutsche Bahn AG** is the national railway of Germany. It offers many domestic and international routes. Tickets can be purchased at the station or through a travel agent. Buy your tickets in advance to get the cheapest fare and to guarantee seating. Many reduced-fare options are available; visit the **Deutsche Bahn AG** website or speak to a travel agent for more information.

Departures

Which track [platform] to...?	**Von welchem Bahnsteig fährt der Zug nach ...?** *fohn vehlkh·ehm bahn·shtieg fehrt dehr tsoog nahkh ...*
Is this the track [platform]/train to...?	**Ist das der Bahnsteig/Zug nach ...?** *ihst dahs dehr bahn·shtieg/tsoog nahkh ...*
Where is platform...?	**Wo ist Bahnsteig ...?** *voh ihst bahn·shtieg ...*
Where do I change for...?	**Wo steige ich um nach ...?** *voh shtieg·uh eekh oom nahkh ...*

On Board

Can I sit here?	**Kann ich mich hier hinsetzen?** *kahn eekh meekh heer hihn·seht·suhn*
Can I open the window?	**Kann ich das Fenster öffnen?** *kahn eekh dahs fehn·stehr erf·nuhn*
Is this seat available?	**Ist der Platz frei?** *ihst dehr plahts frie*
That's my seat.	**Das ist mein Platz.** *dahs ihst mien plahts*
Here's my reservation.	**Hier ist meine Reservierung.** *heer ihst mien·uh reh·sehr·veer·roong*

YOU MAY HEAR...

Bitte einsteigen! *biht·tuh ien·shtieg·uhn*
Die Fahrkarten, bitte.
dee fahr·kahr·tuhn biht·tuh
Sie müssen in ... umsteigen.
zee mews·uhn ihn ... oom·shtieg·uhn
Nächster Halt ... Hauptbahnhof.
nehkh·stehr hahlt ... howpt·bahn·hohf

All aboard!
Tickets, please.

You have to change
at...
Next stop...

Bus

Where's the bus station?	**Wo ist die Bushaltestelle?** *voh ihst dee boos•hahlt•uh•shtehl•uh*
How far is it?	**Wie weit ist es?** *vee viet ihst ehs*
How do I get to…?	**Wie komme ich nach …?** *vee kohm•uh eekh nahk…*
Is this the bus to…?	**Ist das der Bus nach …?** *ihst dahs dehr boos nahkh…*
Can you tell me when to get off?	**Können Sie mir sagen, wann ich aussteigen muss?** *kerhn•uhn zee meer zahg•uhn vahn eekh ows•shtieg•uhn moos*
Do I have to change buses?	**Muss ich umsteigen?** *moos eekh oom•shtieg•uhn*
Stop here, please!	**Bitte halten Sie hier!** *biht•tuh hahlt•uhn zee heer*

For Tickets, see page 19.

Bus and tram stops are marked by a green **H** for **Haltestelle** (stop). Larger cities, such as Berlin, Munich and Hamburg, offer 24-hour service. Service is limited on holidays and weekends. In large German cities, the same ticket or pass can be used for the bus, subway, tram and above-ground train systems. Purchase tickets from the machines at bus stops or subway/tram stations. Check with a local travel agency or tourist information office about special discount tickets and offers.

YOU MAY SEE...

BUSHALTESTELLE	bus stop
STOPP-TASTE	request stop
EINGANG/AUSGANG	enter/exit
FAHRSCHEIN ENTWERTEN	validate your ticket

Abfahrt in

Linie Ziel

M46 U Britz-Süd	4 min
M29 U Hermannplatz	8 min
M19 U Mehringdamm	10 min
M46 U Britz-Süd	11 min
M29 U Hermannplatz	

U-Bahnhof Wittenbergplatz

YOU MAY SEE...

Fahrtziel	destination
Einzelfahrt	one-trip ticket
Tageskarte	day pass
Gruppenkarte	group pass
Wochenkarte	weekly pass

U-Bahn

Where's the U-Bahn [underground] station?	**Wo ist die U-Bahn-Haltestelle?** *voh ihst dee oo•bahn•halt•uh•shtehl•uh*
A map, please.	**Eine Übersichtskarte, bitte.** *ien•nuh ew•behr•zehkhts•kahr•tuh biht•tuh*
Which line for...?	**Welche Linie fährt nach ...?** *vehlkh•uh lihn•ee•uh fehrt nahkh ...*
Which direction?	**Welche Richtung?** *vehlkh•uh reekh•toong*
Do I have to transfer [change]?	**Muss ich umsteigen?** *moos eekh oom•shtieg•uhn*
Is this the U-Bahn [train] to...?	**Ist das die U-Bahn nach ...?** *ihst dahs dee oo•bahn nahkh ...*

| How many stops to...? | **Wie viele Haltestellen sind es bis ...?** *vee feel•uh halt•uh•shtehl•uhn zihnt ehs bihs ...* |
| Where are we? | **Wo sind wir?** *voh zihnt veer* |

For Tickets, see page 19.

All main cities in Germany have an **U-Bahn** (underground/subway), an **S-Bahn** (light rail system, above and below ground) or both. In most cities, the same ticket can be used for the **U-Bahn**, **S-Bahn** and bus and tram lines. Operating times vary for each city, but most operate from 4:00 a.m to midnight or 1:00 a.m. during the week, with some routes offering 24-hour service on weekends.
Most stations feature ticket machines; some may be in English.

Boat & Ferry

When is the ferry to...?	**Wann geht die Fähre nach ...?** *vahn geht dee fehr•uh nahkh ...*
Can I take my car?	**Kann ich mein Auto mitnehmen?** *kahn eekh mien ow•toh miht•nehm•uhn*
What time is the next sailing?	**Wann fährt das nächste Schiff ab?** *vahn fehrt dahs nehkh•ste shihf ahb*
Can I book a seat/cabin?	**Kann ich einen Sitzplatz/eine Kabine reservieren?** *kahn eekh ien•uhn sihts•plahts/ien•uh kah•bee•nuh reh•sehr•veer•uhn*

YOU MAY SEE...

| RETTUNGSBOOT | life boat |
| SCHWIMMWESTE | life jacket |

How long is the crossing?	**Wie lange dauert die Überfahrt?**
	vee lahng·uh dow·ehrt dee ew·behr·fahrt

For Tickets, see page 19.

Ferry service across the Baltic Sea is available between Germany and Denmark, Sweden, Finland and Norway, or across the North Sea to the U.K. Ferry service is also available across Lake Constance to Austria and Switzerland. Boat trips are a fun way to explore the many rivers and lakes throughout Germany. Ferry and boat trips can be arranged by contacting your travel agent or searching the internet.

Taxi

Where can I get a taxi?	**Wo finde ich ein Taxi?** *voh fihnd·uh eekh ien tahk·see*
Can you send a taxi?	**Können Sie ein Taxi schicken?**
	kern·nuhn zee ein tahk·see shihk·uhn

YOU MAY HEAR...

Wohin? *voh·hihn*

Wie ist die Adresse? *wee ihst dee ah·drehs·uh*

Where to?

What's the address?

Es wird ein Nachtzuschlag/ Flughafenzuschlag berechnet.

ehs veerd ien nahkht·tsoo·shlahg/ floog·hahf·uhn·tsoo·shlahg buh·rehkh·nuht

There's a nighttime/ airport surcharge.

You can catch a taxi at taxi stands, by calling to arrange for pick up, or by flagging down a passing available taxi. Taxi stands can be found at train stations, airports, large hotels and other popular areas in the city, such as shopping areas, parks and tourist destinations. Taxi service numbers can be found in the phone book or by asking your hotel concierge. All taxis are metered and will charge a base rate plus a rate per kilometer traveled. To tip the driver, round the fare up to the next euro or two, depending on the service.

Do you have the number for a taxi?	**Haben Sie die Telefonnummer für ein Taxi?** *hah•buhn zee dee tehl•uh•fohn•noom•ehr fewr ien tahk•see*
I'd like a taxi now/ for tomorrow at…	**Ich brauche jetzt/für morgen um … ein Taxi.** *eekh browkh•uh yehtst/fewr mohrg•uhn oom … ien tahk•see*
Pick me up at…	**Holen Sie mich um … ab.** *hohl•uhn zee meekh oom … ahp*
I'm going…	**Ich möchte …** *eekh merkh•tuh …*
to this address	**zu dieser Adresse** *tsoo deez•ehr ah•drehs•suh*
to the airport	**zum Flughafen** *tsoom floog•hah•fuhn*
to the train station	**zum Bahnhof** *tsoom bahn•hohf*
I'm late.	**Ich bin spät dran.** *eekh bihn shpayt drahn*
Can you drive faster/slower?	**Können Sie schneller/langsamer fahren?** *kern•nuhn zee shnehl•ehr/lahng•sahm•ehr fahr•uhn*
Stop here.	**Halten Sie hier an.** *hahl•tuhn zee heer ahn*
Wait here.	**Warten Sie hier.** *vahrt•uhn zee heer*
How much?	**Wie viel kostet es?** *vee feel kohs•tuht ehs*

You said it would cost...	**Sie sagten, es würde ... kosten.**
	zee zahg·tuhn ehs vewrd·uh ... kohs·tuhn
Keep the change.	**Stimmt so.** *shtihmt zoh*
The receipt, please.	**Die Quittung, bitte.** *dee kviht·oong biht·tuh*

Bicycle & Motorbike

I'd like to hire...	**Ich möchte gern ... mieten.** *eekh merkh·tuh gehrn ... meet·uhn*
a bicycle	**ein Fahrrad** *ien fahr·raht*
a moped	**ein Moped** *ien moh·pehd*
a motorbike	**ein Motorrad** *ien moh·tohr·raht*
How much per day/week?	**Wie viel pro Tag/Woche?** *vee feel proh tahk/vohkh·uh*
Can I have a helmet/lock?	**Kann ich einen Helm/ein Schloss haben?** *kahn eekh ien·uhn hehlm/ien shlohs hah·buhn*

Car Hire

Where's the car hire?	**Wo ist die Autovermietung?** *voh ihst dee ow·toh·fehr·miet·oong*
I'd like...	**Ich möchte ...** *eekh merkh·tuh ...*
a cheap/small car	**ein billiges/kleines Auto** *ien bihl·lee·guhs/ klien·uhs ow·toh*
an automatic/ a manual car	**ein Auto mit Automatikschaltung/ Gangschaltung** *ien ow·toh miht ow·toh·mah·teek·shahl·toong/gahng·shahl·toong*
air conditioning	**ein Auto mit Klimaanlage** *ien ow·toh miht klee·mah·ahn·lah·guh*
a car seat	**einen Kindersitz** *ien·uhn kihnd·ehr·zihts*
How much...?	**Wie viel kostet es ...?** *vee feel kohs·tuht ehs ...*
per day/week	**pro Tag/Woche** *proh tahk/vohkh·uh*
per kilometer	**pro Kilometer** *proh kee·loh·meh·tehr*

for unlimited mileage	**mit unbegrenzter Kilometerzahl**
	miht oon•buh•grehnts•tuhr kee•loh•meh•tehr•tsahl
with insurance	**mit Versicherung** *miht fehr•zeekh•ehr•oong*
Are there any discounts?	**Gibt es irgendwelche Ermäßigungen?**
	gihpt ehs eer•guhnd•vehlkh•uh ehr•meh•see•goong•uhn

YOU MAY HEAR...

Haben Sie einen internationalen Führerschein? *hah•buhn zee ien•uh* *ihnt•ehr•nah•syoh•nahl•uhn fewhr•uhr•shien*	Do you have an international driver's license?
Ihren Reisepass, bitte. *eehr•uhn riez•uh•pahs biht•tuh*	Your passport, please.
Möchten Sie eine Versicherung? *merkht•uhn zee ien•uh fehr•seekh•ehr•roong*	Do you want insurance?
Ich benötige eine Anzahlung. *eekh buh•nert•ee•guh ien•uh ahn•tsah•loong*	I'll need a deposit.
Bitte unterschreiben Sie hier. *biht•tuh oont•ehr•shrieb•uhn zee heer*	Sign here, please.

Fuel Station

Where's the fuel station?	**Wo ist die Tankstelle?** *voh ihst dee tahnk•shtehl•luh*
Fill it up, please.	**Bitte volltanken.** *biht•tuh fohl•tahnk•uhn*
. . .euros, please.	**. . . Euro, bitte.** *. . . oy•roh biht•tuh*
I'll pay in cash/by credit card.	**Ich bezahle bar/mit Kreditkarte.** *eekh beht•sahl•uh bahr/miht kreh•deet•kahr•tuh*

YOU MAY SEE...

BENZIN	gas [petrol]
BLEIFREI	unleaded
NORMAL	regular
SUPER	super
DIESEL	diesel

Asking Directions

Is this the way to...? **Ist das der Weg nach ...?**
ihst dahs dehr vehg nahkh ...

How far is it to...? **Wie weit ist es bis ...?** *vee viet ihst ehs bihs ...*

YOU MAY HEAR...

geradeaus *geh·rahd·uh·ows*	straight ahead
links *leenks*	left
rechts *rehkhts*	right
an der/um die Ecke *ahn dehr/oom dee eh·kuh*	on/around the corner
gegenüber *geh·guhn·ew·behr*	opposite
hinter *hihnt·ehr*	behind
neben *nehb·uhn*	next to
nach *nahkh*	after
nördlich/südlich *nerd·leekh/zewd·leekh*	north/south
östlich/westlich *erst·leekh/vehst·leekh*	east/west
an der Ampel *ahn dehr ahmp·ehl*	at the traffic light
an der Kreuzung *ahn dehr kroytz·oong*	at the intersection

Where's...?	**Wo ist ...?** *voh ihst ...*
Street	**die ... Straße** *dee ... shtrahs•suh*
this address	**diese Adresse** *deez•uh ah•drehs•uh*
the highway [motorway]	**die Autobahn** *dee•uh ow•toh•bahn*
Can you show me on the map?	**Können Sie mir das auf der Karte zeigen?** *kern•nuhn zee meer dahs owf dehr kahrt•uh tsieg•uhn*
I'm lost.	**Ich habe mich verfahren.** *eekh hahb•uh meekh fehr•fahr•uhn*

YOU MAY SEE...

(50)	HÖCHSTGESCHWINDIGKEIT	maximum speed limit
	ÜBERHOLVERBOT	no passing
	VERBOT FÜR FAHRZEUGE ALLER ART	all vehicles prohibited
	EINBAHNSTRASSE	one-way street
	KEINE DURCHFAHRT	no entry
STOP	STOPP	stop
	VORFAHRT GEWÄHREN	yield

Parking

Can I park here?	**Kann ich hier parken?**	*kahn eekh heer <u>pahrk</u>•uhn*
Where's...?	**Wo ist ...?**	*voh ihst ...*
the parking garage	**das Parkhaus**	*dahs <u>pahrk</u>•hows*
the parking lot [car park]	**der Parkplatz**	*dehr <u>pahrk</u>•plahts*
the parking meter	**die Parkuhr**	*dee <u>pahrk</u>•oor*
How much...?	**Wie viel kostet es ...?**	*vee feel <u>kohs</u>•tuht ehs ...*
per hour	**pro Stunde**	*proh <u>shtoond</u>•uh*
per day	**pro Tag**	*proh tahk*
for overnight	**über Nacht**	*<u>ew</u>•behr nahkht*

Parking on the street is common in Germany; look for the sign showing a white letter 'P' on a blue background. You may see additional parking instructions located under the sign.

The parking sign with the meter symbol indicates that you can park there for the amount of time shown (in hours - for example, **2 Std.** means 2 hours). Ask your rental car company for a parking disc when you pick up your car. Once parked, turn the dial to indicate the time you parked and put the disc on your dashboard where it is visible.

If you see a **mit Parkschein** sign you must buy a parking ticket from a nearby machine and place it on your dashboard where it is visible. Parking lots and garages are other parking options. Most lots and garages use a self-pay system. When entering, obtain the time-stamped ticket from the machine. Use the machine near the pedestrian entrance to pay for parking; insert your ticket into the machine, pay the amount it displays and then remove the validated ticket. Proceed to your car and insert that ticket into the machine at the exit.

Breakdown & Repair

Where's the garage?	**Wo ist die Autowerkstatt?**
	voh ist dee ow•toh•vehrk•shtaht
My car broke down/ won't start.	**Mein Auto ist kaputt/springt nicht an.**
	mien ow•toh ist kah•poot/shprihngt neekht ahn
Can you fix it (today)?	**Können Sie es (heute) reparieren?**
	kern•nuhn zee ehs (hoy•tuh) reh•pah•reer•uhn
When will it be ready?	**Wann wird es fertig sein?**
	vahn wirt ehs fehr•teekh zien
How much?	**Wie viel kostet es?** *vee feel kohs•tuht ehs*
I have a puncture/ flat tyre (tire)	**Ich habe eine Reifenpanne.** *eekh hah•buh ien•uh rie•fehn•pahn•nuh*

Accidents

There was an accident.	**Es hat einen Unfall gegeben.** *ehs haht ien•uhn oon•fahl guh•geh•buhn*
Call an ambulance/ the police.	**Rufen Sie einen Krankenwagen/die Polizei.** *roof•uhn zee ien•uhn krahnk•uhn•vahg•uhn/ dee poh•lee•tsie*

Places to Stay

ESSENTIAL

Can you recommend a hotel?	**Können Sie ein Hotel empfehlen?**
	ker•nuhn zee ien hoh•tehl ehm•pfeh•luhn
I have a reservation.	**Ich habe eine Reservierung.** *eekh hahb•uh ien•uh rehz•ehr•veer•oong*
My name is…	**Mein Name ist …** *mien nahm•uh ihst …*

Do you have a room…?	**Haben Sie ein Zimmer …?** _hah·buhn zee ien tsihm·mehr …_
for one person/ two people	**für eine Person/zwei Personen** _fewr ien·uh pehr·sohn/tsvie pehr·sohn·uhn_
with a bathroom	**mit Bad** _miht bahd_
with air conditioning	**mit Klimaanlage** _miht kleem·uh·ahn·lahg·uh_
For…	**Für …** _fewr …_
tonight	**heute Nacht** _hoy·tuh nahkht_
two nights	**zwei Nächte** _tsvie nehkht·uh_
one week	**eine Woche** _ien·uh vohkh·uh_
How much?	**Wie viel kostet es?** _vee feel kohs·tuht ehs_
Is there anything cheaper?	**Gibt es etwas Billigeres?** _gihpt ehs eht·vahs bihl·lee·geh·ruhs_
When's check-out?	**Wann ist der Check-out?** _vahn ihst dehr tshehk·owt_
Can I leave this in the safe?	**Kann ich das im Safe lassen?** _kahn eekh dahs ihm sehf lahs·suhn_
Can I leave my bags?	**Kann ich meine Taschen hierlassen?** _kahn eekh mien·uh tahsh·uhn heer·lahs·suhn_
Can I have my bill/a receipt?	**Kann ich meine Rechnung/eine Quittung haben?** _kahn eekh mien·uh rehkh·noong/ ien·uh kveet·oong hah·buhn_
I'll pay in cash/by credit card.	**Ich bezahle bar/mit Kreditkarte.** _eekh beht·sahl·uh bahr/miht kreh·deet·kahr·tuh_

Somewhere to Stay

| Can you recommend…? | **Können Sie … empfehlen?** _kern·uhn zee … ehm·pfeh·luhn_ |
| a hotel | **ein Hotel** _ien hoh·tehl_ |

If you didn't reserve accommodation before your trip, visit the local **Touristeninformationsbüro** (tourist information office) for recommendations on places to stay.

a hostel	**eine Jugendherberge** *ien·uh yoog·uhnd·hehr·behr·guh*
a campsite	**einen Campingplatz** *ien·uhn kahmp·eeng·plahts*
a bed and breakfast	**eine Pension** *ien·uh pehn·syohn*
What is near it?	**Was ist in der Nähe davon?** *vahs ihst ihn dehr neh·uh dah·fohn*
How do I get there?	**Wie komme ich dorthin?** *vee kohm·uh eekh dohrt·hihn*

At the Hotel

I have a reservation.	**Ich habe eine Reservierung.** *eekh hahb·uh ien·uh rehz·ehr·veer·oong*
My name is...	**Mein Name ist ...** *mien nahm·uh ihst ...*
Do you have a room...?	**Haben Sie ein Zimmer ...?** *hah·buhn zee ien tsihm·mehr ...*

Travelers have numerous accommodation options in Germany, from budget to luxury. A **Pension** (bed and breakfast) provides opportunities to experience life in a German home. **Jugendherbergen** (youth hostels) are also available, catering to travelers of all ages. **Urlaub auf dem Bauernhof** (farm stay) is a great way to see the countryside and enjoy rural Germany. In some areas, you may be able to find **Modernisierte Schlossunterkünfte**, old castles that have been converted into beautiful accommodations. **Ferienwohnungen** (vacation apartments) and **Ferienhäuser** (holiday homes) allow travelers to rent fully equipped apartments and villas throughout Germany. All options can be booked with travel agents, tour companies or on the internet.

with a bathroom [toilet]/shower	**mit Bad/Dusche** *miht bahd/doo•shuh*
with air conditioning	**mit Klimaanlage** *miht kleem•uh•ahn•lah•guh*
that's smoking/ non-smoking	**für Raucher/Nichtraucher** *fewr rowkh•ehr/ neekht•rowkh•ehr*
For...	**Für ...** *fewr ...*
tonight	**heute Nacht** *hoyt•uh nahkht*
two nights	**zwei Nächte** *tsvie nehkht•uh*
a week	**eine Woche** *ien•uh vohkh•uh*
Do you have ...?	**Haben Sie ...?** *hah•buhn zee ...*
a computer	**einen Computer** *ien•uhn kohm•pjoot•ehr*
an elevator [a lift]	**einen Fahrstuhl** *ien•uhn fahr•shtoohl*
(wireless) internet service	**(wireless) Internetanschluss** *(wier•luhs) ihnt•ehr•neht•ahn•shloos*

room service	**Zimmerservice** _tsihm·mehr·sehr·vees_
a pool	**einen Pool** _ien·uhn pool_
a gym	**einen Fitnessraum** _ien·uhn fiht·nehs·rowm_
I need…	**Ich brauche …** _eekh browkh·uh …_
an extra bed	**ein zusätzliches Bett**
	ien tsoo·zehts·leeks·uhs beht
a cot	**ein Kinderbett** _ien kihnd·ehr·beht_
a crib	**ein Gitterbett** _ien giht·tehr·beht_

For Numbers, see page 165.

For Numbers, see page 165.

41

YOU MAY HEAR…

Ihren Reisepass/Ihre Kreditkarte, bitte.	Your passport /credit
eehr·uhn riez·uh·pahs/eehr·uh	card, please.
kreh·deet·kahrt·uh biht·tuh	
Bitte füllen Sie dieses Formular aus.	Fill out this form,
biht·tuh fewl·uhn zee deez·uhs fohr·moo·lahr ows	please.
Bitte unterschreiben Sie hier. _biht·tuh_	Sign here, please.
oon·tehr·shrieb·uhn zee heer	

Price

How much per night/week?	**Wie viel kostet es pro Nacht/Woche?**
	vee feel kohs·tuht ehs proh nahkht/vohkh·uh
Does that include breakfast/sales tax [VAT]?	**Beinhaltet der Preis ein Frühstück/ Mehrwertsteuer?** _beh·ien·hahlt·uht dehr_
	pries ien frewh·shtewkh/mehr·wehrt·shtoy·ehr
Are there any discounts?	**Gibt es irgendwelche Ermäßigungen?**
	gihpt ehs eer·guhnd·vehlkh·uh ehr·meh·see·goong·uhn

Preferences

Can I see the room?	**Kann ich das Zimmer sehen?** *kahn eekh dahs <u>tsihm</u>•mehr <u>zeh</u>•uhn*
I'd like a...room.	**Ich möchte ein ... Zimmer.** *eekh <u>merkh</u>•tuh ien ... <u>tsihm</u>•muhr*
better	**besseres** <u>behs</u>•sehr•uhs
bigger	**größeres** <u>grers</u>•ehr•uhs
cheaper	**billigeres** <u>bihl</u>•lee•gehr•uhs
quieter	**ruhigeres** <u>roo</u>•ee•gehr•uhs
I'll take it.	**Ich nehme es.** *eekh <u>nehm</u>•uh ehs*
No, I won't take it.	**Nein, ich nehme es nicht.** *nien eekh <u>nehm</u>•uh ehs neekht*

Questions

Where's...?	**Wo ist ...?** *voh ihhst ...*
the bar	**die Bar** *dee bahr*
the bathroom [toilet]	**die Toilette** *dee toy•<u>leht</u>*
the elevator [lift]	**der Fahrstuhl** *dehr <u>fahr</u>•shtoohl*
Can I have...?	**Kann ich ... haben?** *kahn eekh ... <u>hah</u>•buhn*
a blanket	**eine Decke** <u>ien</u>•uh <u>dehk</u>•uh
an iron	**ein Bügeleisen** *ien <u>bew</u>•guh•liez•ehn*
the room key/the key card	**den Zimmerschlüssel/die Schlüsselkarte** *dehn <u>tsihm</u>•mehr•shlews•uhl/dee <u>shlews</u>•ehl•kahrt•uh*
a pillow	**ein Kissen** *ien <u>kihs</u>•suhn*
soap	**Seife** <u>zief</u>•uh
toilet paper	**Toilettenpapier** *toy•<u>leht</u>•tuhn•pah•peer*
a towel	**ein Handtuch** *ien <u>hahnt</u>•tookh*
Do you have an adapter for this?	**Haben Sie hierfür einen Adapter?** <u>hah</u>•buhn zee heer•<u>fewr</u> <u>ien</u>•uhn ah•<u>dahp</u>•tehr

How do I turn on the lights?	**Wie schalte ich das Licht an?** *vee shahlt·uh eekh dahs leekht ahn*
Can you wake me at…?	**Können Sie mich um … wecken?** *kern·nuhn zee meekh oom … vehk·uhn*
Can I leave this in the safe?	**Kann ich das im Safe lassen?** *kahn eekh dahs ihm sehf lahs·suhn*
Can I have my things from the safe?	**Kann ich meine Sachen aus dem Safe haben?** *kahn eekh mien·uh zahkh·uhn ows dehm sehf hah·buhn*
Is there mail [post]/ a message for me?	**Haben Sie Post/eine Nachricht für mich?** *hah·buhn zee pohst/ien·uh nahkh·reekht fewr meekh*
Do you have a laundry service?	**Bieten Sie einen Wäscheservice?** *bih·tuhn zee ien·uhn vehsh·eh·ser·vice*

Problems

| There's a problem. | **Es gibt ein Problem.** *ehs gihbt ien prohb·lehm* |
| I lost my key/my key card. | **Ich habe meinen Schlüssel/meine Schlüsselkarte verloren.** *eekh hahb·uh mien·uhn shlews·uhl/mien·uh shlews·ehl·kahrt·uh fehr·lohr·uhn* |

YOU MAY SEE…

DRÜCKEN/ZIEHEN	push/pull
TOILETTE	bathroom [toilet]
DUSCHE	shower
FAHRSTUHL	elevator [lift]
TREPPE	stairs
WÄSCHEREI	laundry
BITTE NICHT STÖREN	do not disturb
FEUERSCHUTZTÜR	fire door
NOTAUSGANG	(emergency) exit
WECKRUF	wake-up call

I'm locked out of the room.	**Ich habe mich ausgesperrt.** *eekh hahb•uh meekh ows•guh•shpehrt*
There's no hot water/toilet paper.	**Ich habe kein heißes Wasser/Toilettenpapier.** *eekh hahb•uh kien hies•suhs vahs•sehr/ toy•leht•uhn•pah•peer*
The room is dirty.	**Das Zimmer ist schmutzig.** *dahs tsihm•mehr ihst shmoot•seek*
There are bugs in the room.	**Im Zimmer sind Insekten.** *ihm tsihm•mehr zihnt ihn•sehkt•uhn*
The…doesn't work.	**… funktioniert nicht.** *… foonk•syoh•neert neekht*
Can you fix…?	**Können Sie … reparieren?** *kern•nuhn zee … reh•pah•reer•ruhn*
the air conditioning	**die Klimaanlage** *dee kleem•uh•ahn•lahg•uh*
the fan	**den Ventilator** *dehn vehn•tee•laht•ohr*
the heat [heating]	**die Heizung** *dee hiets•oong*
the light	**das Licht** *dahs leekht*
the TV	**den Fernseher** *dehn fehrn•seh•ehr*
the toilet	**die Toilette** *dee toy•leht•tuh*
I'd like another room.	**Ich möchte gern ein anderes Zimmer.** *eekh merkh•tuh gehrn ien ahn•dehr•uhs tsihm•mehr*

Checking Out

Can I have an itemized bill/ a receipt?	**Kann ich eine aufgeschlüsselte Rechnung/ Quittung haben?** *kahn eekh ien•uh owf•guh•shlews•ehlt•uh rekh•noong/ kveet•oong hah•buhn*

Voltage is 220, and plugs are two-pronged. You may need a converter and/or an adapter for your appliances.

When's check-out?	**Wann ist der Check-out?** *vahn ihst dehr tshehk•owt*
Can I leave my bags here until…?	**Kann ich mein Gepäck bis … hierlassen?** *kahn eekh mien geh•pehk bihs … heer•lahs•uhn*
I think there's a mistake.	**Ich glaube, hier stimmt etwas nicht.** *eekh glowb•uh heer shtihmt eht•vahs neekht*
I'll pay in cash/by credit card.	**Ich bezahle bar/mit Kreditkarte.** *eekh beht•sahl•uh bahr/miht kreh•deet•kahrt•uh*

At hotels, it is common to leave tips for services provided. If you are happy with the housekeeping service, leave a tip of € 1-2 per day for the housekeeper in your room when you leave. Tip porters and your concierge € 2-3 if they provide assistance.

Renting

I reserved an apartment/a room.	**Ich habe ein Apartment/ein Zimmer reserviert.** *eekh hahb•uh ien ah•pahrt•muhnt/ ien tsihm•mehr reh•sehr•veert*
My name is…	**Mein Name ist …** *mien nahm•uh ihst …*
Can I have the keys?	**Kann ich den Schlüssel haben?** *kahn eekh dehn shlews•suhl hah•buhn*
Are there…?	**Gibt es …?** *gihpt ehs …*
dishes	**Geschirr** *guh•sheer*
pillows	**Kissen** *kihs•suhn*
sheets	**Bettwäsche** *beht•vehsh•uh*
towels	**Handtücher** *hahnt•tewkh•ehr*
kitchen utensils	**Haushaltsgeräte** *hows•hahlts•guh•reht•uh*
When do I put out the bins/recycling?	**Wann stelle ich den Abfall/Müll raus?** *vahn shtehl•luh eekh dehn ahp•fahl/mewl rows*

...is broken.	**... funktioniert nicht.**	... foonk•syoh•_neert_ neekht
How does...work?	**Wie funktioniert ...?**	vee foonk•syoh•_neert_ ...
the air conditioner	**die Klimaanlage** dee _kleem_•uh•ahn•lahg•uh	
the dishwasher	**die Spülmaschine** dee _shpewl_•mah•sheen•uh	
the freezer	**der Gefrierschrank** dehr guh•_freer_•shrahnk	
the heating	**die Heizung** dee _hiet_•soong	
the microwave	**die Mikrowelle** dee mee•kroh•_vehl_•luh	
the refrigerator	**der Kühlschrank** dehr _kewhl_•shrahnk	
the stove	**der Herd** dehr hehrd	
the washing machine	**die Waschmaschine** dee _vahsh_•mah•shee•nuh	

Domestic Items

I need...	**Ich brauche ...** eekh _browkh_•uh ...	
an adapter	**einen Adapter** _ien_•uhn ah•_dahp_•tehr	
aluminum [kitchen] foil	**Alufolie** ah•loo•_foh_•lee•uh	
a bottle opener	**einen Flaschenöffner** _ien_•uhn _flahsh_•uhn•erf•nehr	
a broom	**einen Besen** _ien_•uhn _behz_•uhn	
a can opener	**einen Dosenöffner** _ien_•uhn _doh_•suhn•erf•nehr	
cleaning supplies	**Reinigungsmittel** _rien_•ee•goongs•miht•tuhl	
a corkscrew	**einen Korkenzieher** _ien_•uhn _kohrk_•uhn•tsee•ehr	
detergent	**Waschmittel** _vahsh_•miht•tuhl	
dishwashing liquid	**Geschirrspülmittel** guh•_sheer_•shpewl•miht•tuhl	
bin bags	**Abfallsäcke** _ahb_•fahl•seh•khuh	
a lightbulb	**eine Glühbirne** _ien_•uh _glewh_•beer•nuh	
matches	**Streichhölzer** _shtriekh_•herlt•sehr	
a mop	**einen Wischmopp** _ien_•uhn _vihsh_•mohp	
napkins	**Servietten** sehr•_vyeht_•tuhn	
paper towels	**Küchenrollen** _kewkh_•uhn•rohl•luhn	

plastic wrap [cling film]	**Frischhaltefolie** _frihsh_•hahl•tuh•foh•lee•uh	
a plunger	**eine Saugglocke** _ien_•uh _zowg_•lohk•uh	
scissors	**eine Schere** _ien_•uh _shehr_•uh	
a vacuum cleaner	**einen Staubsauger** _ien_•uhn _shtowb_•sowg•ehr	

For In the Kitchen, see page 77.

For Oven Temperatures, see page 171.

At the Hostel

Is there a bed available?	**Haben Sie ein Bett frei?** _hah_•buhn zee ien beht frie
Can I have...?	**Kann ich ... haben?** kahn eekh ... _hah_•buhn
a single/double room	**ein Einzelzimmer/Doppelzimmer** ien _ient_•sehl•tsihm•mehr/_dohp_•pehl•tsihm•muhr
a blanket	**eine Decke** _ien_•uh _dehk_•huh
a pillow	**ein Kissen** ien _kihs_•suhn
sheets	**Bettwäsche** _beht_•vehsh•uh
a towel	**ein Handtuch** ien _hahnt_•tookh

There are more than 500 hostels throughout Germany, in cities large and small and in rural locations. You may need a Hostelling International membership card to stay at these hostels, many of which belong to **Deutsches Jugendherbergswerk (DJV)**. Hostels are inexpensive accommodations that offer dormitory-style rooms and, sometimes, private or semi-private rooms. Some offer private bathrooms, though most have shared facilities. There is usually a self-service kitchen on site. Booking in advance is a good idea, especially in large cities during festivals or holidays. Reservations can be made over the phone or online. Visit the Hostelling International website for more information.

Do you have lockers?	**Haben Sie Schließfächer?** _hah_·buhn zee _shlees_·fehkh·ehr
When do you lock up?	**Wann schließen Sie ab?** vahn _shlees_·suhn zee ahp
Do I need a membership card?	**Brauche ich eine Mitgliedskarte?** _browkh_·uh eekh _ien_·uh _miht_·gleeds·kahrt·uh
Here's my international student card.	**Hier ist mein internationaler Studentenausweis.** heer ihst mien ihn·tehr·nah·syoh·_nahl_·ehr shtoo·_dehnt_·uhn·ows·vies

Going Camping

Can I camp here?	**Kann ich hier campen?** kahn eekh heer _kahmp_·uhn
Where's the campsite?	**Wo ist der Campingplatz?** voh ihst dehr _kahmp_·eeng·plahts
What is the charge per day/week?	**Was kostet es pro Tag/Woche?** vahs _kohst_·uht ehs proh tahk/_vohkh_·uh
Are there ...?	**Gibt es ...?** gihpt ehs ...
cooking facilities	**Kochmöglichkeiten** _kohkh_·merg·leekh·kiet·uhn
electric outlets	**Steckdosen** _shtehk_·dohz·uhn
laundry facilities	**Waschmaschine** _vahsh_·maksch·een·uh
showers	**Duschen** _doosh_·uhn
tents for hire	**Mietzelte** _meet_·tsehl·tuh
Where can I empty the chemical toilet?	**Wo kann ich die Campingtoilette leeren?** voh kahn eekh dee _kahmp_·eeng·toy·leh·tuh _lehr_·uhn

For Domestic Items, see page 46.

For In the Kitchen, see page 77.

> ### YOU MAY SEE...
> | **TRINKWASSER** | drinking water |
> | **ZELTEN VERBOTEN** | no camping |
> | **OFFENES FEUER VERBOTEN** | no fires |

Communications

ESSENTIAL

Where's an internet cafe?	**Wo gibt es ein Internetcafé?** *voh gihpt ehs ien ihnt·ehr·neht·kah·feh*
Can I access the internet/check e-mail?	**Kann ich das Internet benutzen/meine E-Mails lesen?** *kahn eekh dahs ihnt·ehr·neht beh·noot·suhn/mien·uh ee·miels lehz·uhn*
How much per (half) hour?	**Wie viel kostet eine (halbe) Stunde?** *vee feel kohst·uht ien·uh (hahlb·uh) shtoond·uh*
How do I log on?	**Wie melde ich mich an?** *vee mehld·uh eekh meekh ahn*
A phone card, please.	**Eine Telefonkarte, bitte.** *ien·uh tehl·uh·fohn·kahrt·uh biht·tuh*
Can I have your phone number?	**Kann ich Ihre Telefonnummer haben?** *kahn eekh eehr·uh tehl·uh·fohn·noom·ehr hah·buhn*
Here's my number/e-mail.	**Hier ist meine Telefonnummer/E-Mail.** *heer ihst mien·uh tehl·uh·fohn·noom·ehr/ee·miel*
Call me.	**Rufen Sie mich an.** *roo·fuhn zee meekh ahn*
E-mail me.	**Mailen Sie mir.** *miel·uhn zee meer*
Hello. This is…	**Hallo. Hier ist …** *hah·loh heer ihst …*
Can I speak to…?	**Kann ich mit … sprechen?** *kahn eekh miht … shprehkh·uhn*
Can you repeat that, please?	**Könnten Sie das bitte wiederholen?** *kern·tuhn zee dahs biht·tuh veed·ehr·hohl·uhn*
I'll call back later.	**Ich rufe später zurück.** *eekh roof·uh shpeht·ehr tsoo·rewkh*
Bye.	**Auf Wiederhören.** *owf veed·ehr·her·ruhn*

| Where's the post office? | **Wo ist die Post?** *voh ihst dee pohst* |
| I'd like to send this to... | **Ich möchte das nach ... schicken.** *eekh merkh-tuh dahs nahkh ... shihk-uhn* |

Online

Where's an internet cafe?	**Wo gibt es ein Internetcafé?** *voh gihpt ehs ien ihnt-ehr-neht-kah-feh*
Does it have wireless internet?	**Gibt es dort wireless Internet?** *gihpt ehs dohrt wier-luhs ihnt-ehr-neht*
What is the WiFi password?	**Wie lautet das WLAN-Passwort?** *vee low-teht dahs veh-lahn-pahs-vohrt*
Is the WiFi free?	**Ist der WLAN-Zugang gratis?** *ihst dehr veh-lahn-tsoo-gahng grah-tihs*
Do you have bluetooth?	**Haben Sie Bluetooth?** *hah-buhn zee bloo-tooth*
How do I turn the computer on/off?	**Wie schalte ich den Computer an/aus?** *vee shahlt-uh eekh dehn kohm-pjoot-ehr ahn/ows*
Can I ...?	**Kann ich ...?** *kahn eekh ...*
access the internet	**das Internet benutzen** *dahs ihnt-ehr-neht beh-noot-suhn*
check e-mail	**E-Mails lesen** *ee-miels lehz-uhn*
print	**drucken** *drook-uhn*
plug in/charge my laptop/iPhone/iPad/BlackBerry?	**meinen Laptop/mein iPhone/iPad/BlackBerry aufladen?** *kahn eekh mien-uhn lap-top/mien iphone/ipad/blackberry owf-lahd-uhn*
access Skype?	**Skype verwenden?** *skype fuhr- vehn- dehn*
use any computer	**einen Computer benutzen** *ien-uhn kohm-pjoot-ehr beh-noot-suhn*
How much per (half) hour?	**Wie viel kostet eine (halbe) Stunde?** *vee feel kohst-uht ien-uh (hahlb-uh) shtoond-uh*

How…?	**Wie …?** *vee …*
do I connect	**stelle ich eine Verbindung her** *shteh·luh eekh ien·uh fuhr·bihnd·oong hehr*
do I disconnect	**trenne ich eine Verbindung** *trehn·uh eekh ien·uh fuhr·bihnd·oong*
do I log on/off	**melde ich mich an/ab** *mehld·uh eekh meekh ahn/ahp*
do I type this symbol	**gebe ich dieses Zeichen ein** *geh·buh eekh deez·uhs tsiekh·ehn ien*
What's your e-mail?	**Wie ist Ihre E-Mail-Adresse?** *vee ihst eehr·uh ee·miel·ah·drehs·uh*
My e-mail is…	**Meine E-Mail-Adresse ist …** *mien·uh ee·miel·ah·drehs·uh ihst …*
Do you have a scanner?	**Haben Sie einen Scanner?** *hah·buhn zee ien·uhn scan·nuhr*

Social Media

Are you on Facebook/Twitter?	**Sind Sie bei Facebook/Twitter?** (polite form) *zihnt zee by face·book/twit·ter*
	Bist du bei Facebook/Twitter? (informal form) *bihst doo by face·book/twit·ter*

YOU MAY SEE...

SCHLIESSEN	close
LÖSCHEN	delete
E-MAIL	e-mail
BEENDEN	exit
HILFE	help
INSTANT MESSENGER	instant messenger
INTERNET	internet
ANMELDEN	login
NEUE NACHRICHT	new message
AN/AUS	on/off
ÖFFNEN	open
DRUCKEN	print
SPEICHERN	save
SENDEN	send
BENUTZERNAME/PASSWORT	username/password
WIRELESS INTERNET	wireless internet

What's your user name?	**Was ist Ihr Benutzername? (polite form)** *vahs ihst eehr beh•noots•uhr•nah•muh*
	Was ist dein Benutzername? (informal form) *vahs ihst dien beh•noots•uhr•nah•muh*
I'll follow you on Twitter.	**Ich werde Ihre Twitter-Einträge verfolgen. (polite form)** *eekh vehr•duh eer•he twit•ter•ien•treh•ghe fehr•folg•hun*
	Ich werde deine Twitter-Einträge verfolgen. (informal form) *eekh vehr•duh die•nuh twit•ter•ien•treh•ghe fehr•folg•hun*
Are you following...?	**Verfolgen Sie ...? (polite form)** *fehr•folg•hun zee ...*
	Verfolgst du ...? (informal form) *fehr•folgst doo ...*

I'll add you as a friend.	**Ich werde Sie als Freund/Freundin hinzufügen.** (polite form) *eekh vehrd•uh zee ahls froynd/ froyn•dihn hihn•tsoo•few•guhn*
	Ich werde dich als Freund/Freundin hinzufügen. (informal form) *eekh vehrd•uh deekh ahls froynd/ froyn•dihn hihn•tsoo•few•guhn*
I'll put the pictures on Facebook/Twitter.	**Ich werde die Fotos auf Facebook/Twitter hochladen.** *eekh vehr•duh dee foh•tohs owf face•book/ twit•ter hokh•lah•duhn*
I'll tag you in the pictures.	**Ich werde Sie auf den Fotos markieren.** (polite form) *eekh vehr•duh zee owf dehn foh•tohs mahr•kih•ruhn*
	Ich werde dich auf den Fotos markieren. (informal form) *eekh vehr•duh deekh owf dehn foh•tohs mahr•kih•ruhn*

Phone

A phone card, please	**Eine Telefonkarte, bitte.** *ien•uh tehl•eh•fohn•kahrt•uh biht•tuh*
A prepaid phone please	**Ein Prepaid-Handy, bitte.** *ien pree•paid han•dee biht•tuh*
An international phonecard for...	**Eine internationale Telefonkarte für ...** *ien•uh ihnt•ehr•nah•syoh•nahl•uh tehl•uh•fohn•kahrt•uh fewr ...*
Australia	**Australien** *ow•shtrah•lee•ehn*
Canada	**Kanada** *kah•nah•dah*
Ireland	**Irland** *eer•lahnt*
the U.K.	**Großbritannien** *grohs•bree•tahn•ee•ehn*
the U.S.	**die USA** *dee oo•ehs•ah*
How much?	**Wie viel kostet es?** *vee feel kohs•tuht ehs*

Where's the pay phone?	**Wo ist das Münztelefon?**
	voh ihst dahs mewnts•tehl•uh•fohn
What's the area code/country code for...?	**Was ist die Ortsvorwahl/Landesvorwahl für ...?**
	vahs ihst dee ohrts•fohr•vahl/ lahnd•uhs•fohr•vahl fewr ...
What's the number for Information?	**Was ist die Nummer für die Auskunft?**
	vahs ihst dee noom•ehr fewr dee ows•kuhnft
I'd like the number for...	**Ich hätte gern die Nummer für ...**
	eekh heht•uh gehrn dee noom•ehr fewr ...

YOU MAY HEAR...

Ruff an? *roof ahn*	Who's calling?
Einen Moment, bitte.	Hold on, please.
ien•uhn moh•mehnt biht•tuh	
Ich verbinde Sie. *eekh fehr•bihnd•uh zee*	I'll put you through.
Er *m* /Sie *f* ist nicht da/spricht gerade.	He/She is not here/ on another line.
ehr/zee ihst neekht dah/shpreekht geh•rahd•uh	
Möchten Sie eine Nachricht hinterlassen?	Would you like to leave a message?
merkh•tuhn zee ien•uh nahkh•reekht hihnt•ehr•lahs•suhn	
Bitte rufen Sie später/in zehn Minuten zurück. *biht•tuh roof•uhn zee shpeht•ehr/ihn tsehn mee•noot•uhn tsoo•rewkh*	Please call back later/in ten minutes.
Kann er *m* /sie *f* zurückrufen?	Can he/she call you back?
khan ehr/zee tsoo•rewkh•roof•uhn	
Was ist Ihre Nummer?	What's your number?
vahs ihst eehr•uh noom•ehr	

German public phones are mainly card operated. Phone cards in various amounts can be purchased at newsstands, supermarkets and other shops.

Important telephone numbers include:

Police 110
Fire 112
Ambulance 115
National Directory 11833
National Directory (in English) 11837
International Directory 11834

To call the U.S. or Canada from Germany, dial 001 + area code + phone number. To call the U.K. from Germany, dial 0044 + area code (minus the first 0) + phone number.

I'd like to call collect [reverse the charges].	**Ich möchte ein R-Gespräch führen.** *eekh merkh•tuh ien ehr•guh•shprehkh fewhr•uhn*
My phone doesn't work here.	**Mein Telefon funktioniert hier nicht.** *mien tehl•leh•fohn foonk•syoh•neert heer neekht*
What network are you on?	**Welches Netz nutzen Sie?** *vehl•khehs nehts noot•suhn zee*
Is it 3G?	**Ist es ein 3G-Netz?** *ihst ehs ien drie•geh•nehts*
I have run out of credit/minutes.	**Ich habe kein Guthaben mehr.** *eekh hah•buh kien goot•hah•buhn mehr*
Can I buy some credit?	**Kann ich eine Guthabenkarte kaufen?** *kahn eekh ie•nuh goot•hah•buhn•kahr•tuh kow•fuhn*
Do you have a phone charger?	**Haben Sie ein Handy-Ladegerät?** *hah•buhn zee ien han•dee•lah•duh•guh•reht*
Can I recharge this phone?	**Kann ich dieses Telefon wieder aufladen?** *kahn eekh deez•uhs tehl•uh•fohn veed•ehr owf•lahd•uhn*

Can I have your number, please?	**Können Sie mir bitte Ihre Nummer geben?** _kern_•uhn zee meer _biht_•tuh _eehr_•uh _noom_•ehr _gehb_•uhn
Here's my number.	**Hier ist meine Nummer.** heer ihst _mien_•uh _noom_•ehr
Please call me.	**Bitte rufen Sie mich an.** _biht_•tuh _roof_•uhn zee meekh ahn
Please text me.	**Bitte schicken Sie mir eine SMS.** _bit_•tuh _shihk_•uhn zee meer _ien_•uh _ehs_•ehm•ehs
I'll call you.	**Ich werde Sie anrufen.** eekh _vehrd_•uh zee _ahn_•roof•uhn
I'll text you.	**Ich werde Ihnen eine SMS schicken.** eekh _vehrd_•uh _eehn_•uhn _ien_•uh _ehs_•ehm•ehs _shihk_•uhn

Telephone Etiquette

Hello. This is…	**Hallo. Hier ist …** _hahl_•loh heer ihst …
Can I speak to…?	**Kann ich mit … sprechen?** kahn eekh miht … _shprehkh_•uhn
Extension…	**Durchwahl …** _doorkh_•vahl …
Speak louder/more slowly, please.	**Bitte sprechen Sie lauter/langsamer.** _biht_•tuh _shprehkh_•uhn zee _lowt_•ehr/_lahng_•sahm•ehr
Can you repeat that, please?	**Könnten Sie das bitte wiederholen?** _kern_•tuhn zee dahs _biht_•tuh vee•_dehr_•_hohl_•uhn
I'll call back later.	**Ich rufe später zurück.** eekh _roof_•uh _shpeht_•ehr _tsoo_•rewk
Bye.	**Auf Wiederhören.** owf _veed_•ehr•her•ruhn

For Business Travel, see page 137.

Fax

Can I send/receive a fax here?	**Kann ich hier ein Fax senden/empfangen?** kahn eekh heer ien fahks _zehnd_•uhn/_ehm_•pfahng•uhn
What's the fax number?	**Was ist die Faxnummer?** vahs ihst dee _fahks_•noom•ehr
Please fax this to…	**Bitte faxen Sie das nach …** _biht_•tuh _fahks_•uhn zee dahs nahkh …

YOU MAY HEAR...

Bitte füllen Sie das Zollformular aus. *biht•tuh fewl•luhn zee dahs tsohl•fohr•moo•lahr ows*	Fill out the customs declaration form, please.
Wie viel ist es wert? *vee feel ihst ehs vehrt*	What's the value?
Was ist der Inhalt? *vahs ihst dehr ihn•hahlt*	What's inside?

Post

Where's the post office/mailbox?	**Wo ist die Post/der Briefkasten?** *voh ihst dee pohst/dehr breef•kahs•tuhn*
A stamp for this postcard/letter to..., please.	**Eine Briefmarke für diese Postkarte/ diesen Brief nach ... bitte.** *ien•uh breef•mahrk•uh fewr deez•uh pohst•kahrt•uh/ deez•uhn breef nahkh ... biht•tuh*
How much?	**Wie viel kostet das?** *vee feel kohs•tuht dahs*
Please send this package by airmail/express.	**Senden Sie dieses Paket bitte per Luftpost/Express.** *zehnd•uhn zee deez•uhs pah•keht biht•tuh pehr looft•pohst/ehks•prehs*
A receipt, please.	**Eine Quittung, bitte.** *ien•uh kveet•toong biht•tu*

In addition to mailing options, German post offices offer a variety of other services. Most provide banking services and allow you to deposit or withdraw money and apply for a credit card. On weekdays, post offices are usually open from 8:30 a.m. to 1:00 p.m., and again from 2:30 p.m. to 4:00 p.m. (in larger cities to 6:30 p.m.). On Saturdays they are open from 8:30 a.m. to 1:00 p.m.

Food & Drink

Eating Out	59
Meals & Cooking	67
Drinks	79
On the Menu	83

Eating Out

ESSENTIAL

Can you recommend a good restaurant/bar?	**Können Sie ein gutes Restaurant/eine gute Bar empfehlen?** _ker_·nuhn zee ien _goo_·tuhs reh·stow·_rahnt_/_ien_·uh _goo_·tuh bahr ehm·_pfeh_·luhn
Is there a traditional German/an inexpensive restaurant nearby?	**Gibt es in der Nähe ein typisch deutsches/preisgünstiges Restaurant?** _gihpt ehs ihn dehr _neh_·uh ien _tew_·peesh _doy_·chuhs/_pries_·gewn·stee·guhs reh·stow·_rahnt_
A table for..., please.	**Bitte einen Tisch für ...** _biht_·tuh _ien_·uhn tihsh fewr ...
Can we sit...?	**Können wir ... sitzen?** _ker_·nuhn veer ... _ziht_·tsuhn
here/there	**hier/dort** heer/dohrt
outside	**draußen** _drow_·suhn
in a non-smoking area	**in einem Nichtraucherbereich** ihn _ien_·uhm neekht·_row_·khehr·beh·riehk
I'm waiting for someone.	**Ich warte auf jemanden.** eekh _vahr_·tuh owf _yeh_·mahnd·uhn
Where are the toilets?	**Wo ist die Toilette?** voh ihst dee toy·_leh_·tuh
A menu, please.	**Die Speisekarte, bitte.** dee _shpie_·zuh·kahr·tuh _biht_·tuh
What do you recommend?	**Was empfehlen Sie?** vahs ehm·_pfeh_·luhn zee
I'd like...	**Ich möchte ...** eekh _merkh_·tuh ...
Some more..., please.	**Etwas mehr ..., bitte.** _eht_·vahs mehr ... _biht_·tuh
Enjoy your meal!	**Guten Appetit!** _goo_·tuhn ah·puh·_teet_

The check [bill], please.	**Die Rechnung, bitte.** *dee <u>rehkh</u>•noonk <u>biht</u>•tuh*
Is service included?	**Ist die Bedienung im Preis enthalten?**
	ihsht dee buh•<u>dee</u>•nung ihm pries <u>ehnt</u>•hahl•tuhn
Can I pay by credit card/have a receipt?	**Kann ich mit Kreditkarte bezahlen/eine Quittung haben?** *kahn eekh miht kreh•<u>deet</u>•kahr•tuh beht•<u>sahl</u>•uhn/ien•uh <u>kvee</u>•toonk <u>hah</u>•buhn*
Thank you!	**Danke!** <u>*dahn*</u>•*kuh*

Where to Eat

Can you recommend...?	**Können Sie ... empfehlen?** <u>*ker*</u>•*nuhn zee ...* *ehm•<u>pfeh</u>•luhn*
a restaurant	**ein Restaurant** *ien reh•stow•<u>rahnt</u>*
a bar	**eine Bar** <u>*ien*</u>•*uh bahr*
a cafe	**ein Café** *ien kah•<u>feh</u>*
a fast-food place	**ein Schnellrestaurant** *ien <u>shnehl</u>•reh•stow•rahnt*
a snack bar	**einen Imbiss** <u>*ien*</u>•*uhn <u>ihm</u>•bees*
a cheap restaurant	**ein billiges Restaurant** *ien bihl•lee•guhs reh•stow•rahnt*

an expensive restaurant	**ein teures Restaurant** *ien toy·rehs reh·stow·rahnt*
a restaurant with a good view	**ein Restaurant mit schöner Aussicht** *ien reh·stow·rahnt miht sher·nuhr ows·seekht*
an authentic/ a non-touristy restaurant	**ein authentisches/ein nicht so touristisches Restaurant** *ien ow·tehn·tih·shuhs/ien neekht zoh tou·rihs·tih·shuhs reh·stow·rahnt*

Reservations & Preferences

I'd like to reserve a table…	**Ich möchte einen Tisch … reservieren** *eekh merkh·tuh ien·uhn tihsh … reh·zuh·veer·ehn*
for two	**für zwei Personen** *fewr tsvie pehr·zohn·uhn*
for this evening	**für heute Abend** *fewr hoy·tuh ah·behnt*
for tomorrow at…	**für morgen um …** *fewr mohr·guhn oom …*
A table for two, please.	**Bitte einen Tisch für zwei.** *biht·tuh ien·uhn tihsh fewr tsvie*

YOU MAY HEAR…

Haben Sie eine Reservierung? *hah·buhn zee ien·uh reh·zuh·veer·uhng*
Do you have a reservation?

Für wie viele Personen? *fewr vee fee·luh pehr·zohn·uhn*
For how many people?

Raucher oder Nichtraucher? *row·khuhr oh·duhr neekht·row·khuhr*
Smoking or non-smoking?

Möchten Sie jetzt bestellen? *merkh·tuhn zee yehtst buh·shteh·luhn*
Are you ready to order?

Was möchten Sie? *vahs merkh·tuhn zee*
What would you like?

Ich empfehle … *eekh ehm·pfeh·luh …*
I recommend…

Guten Appetit. *goo·tuhn ah·puh·teet*
Enjoy your meal.

We have a reservation.	**Wir haben eine Reservierung.** *veer* <u>*hah*</u>*-buhn* <u>*ien*</u>*-uh reh-zuh-*<u>*veer*</u>*-uhng*	
My name is…	**Mein Name ist …** *mien* <u>*nahm*</u>*-uh ihst …*	
Can we sit…?	**Können wir … sitzen?** <u>*ker*</u>*-nuhn veer …* <u>*ziht*</u>*-tsuhn*	
here/there	**hier/dort** *heer/dohrt*	
outside	**draußen** <u>*drow*</u>*-suhn*	
in a non-smoking area	**in einem Nichtraucherbereich** *ihn* <u>*ien*</u>*-uhm* <u>*neekht*</u>*-row-khuhr-beh-riekh*	
by the window	**am Fenster** *ahm* <u>*fehn*</u>*-stehr*	
in the shade	**im Schatten** *ihm shaht-tehn*	
in the sun	**in der Sonne** *ihn dehr sohn-nuh*	
Where are the toilets?	**Wo ist die Toilette?** *voh ihst dee toy-*<u>*leh*</u>*-tuh*	

How to Order

Waiter/Waitress!	**Bedienung!** *buh-*<u>*dee*</u>*-nounk*	
We're ready to order.	**Wir möchten bitte bestellen.** *weer* <u>*merkh*</u>*-tuhn* <u>*biht*</u>*-tuh buh-*<u>*shteh*</u>*-luhn*	
May I see the wine list, please?	**Die Weinkarte, bitte.** *dee* <u>*vien*</u>*-kahr-tuh* <u>*biht*</u>*-tuh*	
I'd like…	**Ich möchte …** *eekh* <u>*merhk*</u>*-tuh …*	
a bottle of…	**eine Flasche …** <u>*ien*</u>*-uh* <u>*flah*</u>*-shuh …*	
a carafe of…	**eine Karaffe …** <u>*ien*</u>*-uh kah-*<u>*rah*</u>*-fuh …*	
a glass of…	**ein Glas …** *ien glahs …*	
The menu, please.	**Die Speisekarte, bitte.** *dee* <u>*shpie*</u>*-zuh-kahr-tuh* <u>*biht*</u>*-tuh*	
Do you have…?	**Haben Sie …?** <u>*hah*</u>*-buhn zee …*	
a menu in English	**eine Speisekarte in Englisch** <u>*ien*</u>*-uh* <u>*shpie*</u>*-zuh-kahr-tuh ihn* <u>*ehn*</u>*-gleesh*	
a fixed-price menu	**ein Festpreismenü** *ien* <u>*fehst*</u>*-pries-meh-new*	
a children's menu	**ein Kindermenü** *ien* <u>*kihn*</u>*-dehr-meh-new*	
What do you recommend?	**Was empfehlen Sie?** *vahs ehm-*<u>*pfeh*</u>*-luhn zee*	

What's this?	**Was ist das?** *vahs ihsht dahs*	
What's in it?	**Was ist darin?** *vahs ihsht dah·rihn*	
Is it spicy?	**Ist es scharf?** *ihsht ehs shahrf*	
I'd like…	**Ich möchte gern …** *eekh merkh·tuh gehrn …*	
More…, please.	**Mehr …, bitte.** *mehr … biht·tuh*	
With/Without…	**Mit/Ohne …** *miht/oh·nuh …*	
I can't eat…	**Ich vertrage kein/keine …** *eekh fehr·trah·guh kien/kien·uh …*	
rare	**roh** *roh*	
medium	**medium** *meh·dee·uhm*	
well-done	**durchgebraten** *doorkh·geh·brah·tuhn*	
Without…, please.	**Ohne …, bitte.** *oh·nuh … biht·tuh*	
It's to go [take away], please.	**Bitte zum Mitnehmen.** *biht·tuh tsoom miht·neh·muhn*	

For Drinks, see page 79.

For Negations, see page 161.

YOU MAY SEE…

SPEISEKARTE	menu
TAGESMENÜ	menu of the day
SPEZIALITÄTEN	specials

Cooking Methods

baked	**gebacken** *guh·bahkh·uhn*
boiled	**gekocht** *guh·kohkht*
braised	**geschmort** *guh·shmohrt*
breaded	**paniert** *pah·neert*
creamed	**püriert** *pew·reert*
diced	**gewürfelt** *guh·vewr·fuhlt*

filleted	**filetiert** *fee·luh·teert*
fried	**gebraten** *guh·brah·tuhn*
grilled	**gegrillt** *guh·grihlt*
poached	**pochiert** *poh·sheert*
roasted	**geröstet** *guh·rer·stuht*
sautéed	**sautiert** *zow·teert*
smoked	**geräuchert** *guh·roy·khuhrt*
steamed	**gedünstet** *guh·dewn·stuht*
stewed	**geschmort** *guh·shmohrt*
stuffed	**gefüllt** *guh·fewlt*

Dietary Requirements

I'm...	**Ich bin ...** *eekh bihn ...*
diabetic	**Diabetiker** *dee·ah·beh·tee·kehr*
lactose intolerant	**laktoseintolerant** *lahk·thoh·suh·een·tho·luh·rahnt*
vegetarian	**Vegetarier** *veh·guh·tah·ree·ehr*
vegan	**Veganer** *veh·gah·nehr*
I'm allergic to...	**Ich bin allergisch auf ...** *eekh bihn ah·lehr·geesh owf ...*
I can't eat...	**Ich kann ... essen.** *eekh kahn ... eh·zuhn*
dairy products	**keine Milchprodukte** *kien·uh meelkh·proh·dook·tuh*
gluten	**kein Gluten** *kien gloo·tuhn*
nuts	**keine Nüsse** *kien·uh new·suh*
pork	**kein Schweinefleisch** *kien shvie·nuh·fliesh*
shellfish	**keine Schalentiere** *kien·uh shah·luhn·tee·ruh*
spicy foods	**keine scharf gewürzten Speisen** *kien·uh shahrf guh·vewrt·stuhn shpie·zuhn*
wheat	**kein Weizen** *kien vie·tsuhn*
Is it halal/kosher?	**Ist es halal/koscher?** *ihsht ehs hah·lahl/koh·shuhr*
Do you have...?	**Haben Sie...?** *hah·buhn zee*
skimmed milk	**Magermilch** *mah·guhr·meelkh*

| whole milk | **Vollmilch** *foll•meelkh* |
| soya milk | **Sojamilch** *soh•yah•meelkh* |

Dining with Children

Do you have children's portions?	**Haben Sie Kinderportionen?** <u>hah</u>•buhn zee <u>kihn</u>•dehr•pohr•syoh•nuhn
Can I have a highchair/ child's seat?	**Einen Kindersitz/Kinderstuhl, bitte.** <u>ien</u>•uhn <u>kihnd</u>•ehr•zihtz/<u>kihn</u>•dehr•shtuhl <u>biht</u>•tuh
Where can I feed/ change the baby?	**Wo kann ich das Baby füttern/wickeln?** voh kahn eekh dahs <u>beh</u>•bee few•tuhrn/<u>vihk</u>•uhln
Can you warm this?	**Können Sie das warm machen?** <u>ker</u>•nuhn zee dahs vahrm <u>mah</u>•khuhn

For Traveling with Children, see page 140.

How to Complain

When will our food be ready?	**Wie lange dauert es noch mit dem Essen?** vee <u>lahng</u>•uh <u>dow</u>•ehrt ehs nohkh miht dehm <u>eh</u>•suhn
We can't wait any longer.	**Wir können nicht mehr länger warten.** veer <u>ker</u>•nuhn neekht mehr <u>lehng</u>•ehr <u>vahr</u>•tuhn
We're leaving.	**Wir gehen jetzt.** veer <u>geh</u>•ehn yehtst
I didn't order this.	**Das habe ich nicht bestellt.** dahs <u>hah</u>•buh eekh neekht buh•<u>shtehlt</u>
I ordered...	**Ich habe ... bestellt.** eekh <u>hah</u>•buh ... buh•<u>shtehlt</u>
I can't eat this.	**Ich kann das nicht essen.** eekh kahn dahs neekht <u>eh</u>•suhn
This is too...	**Das ist zu ...** dahs ihst tsoo ...
cold/hot	**kalt/heiß** kahlt/hies
salty/spicy	**salzig/scharf gewürzt** <u>sahl</u>•tseek/shahrf <u>guh</u>•vewrts
tough/bland	**zäh/fad** tseh/fahd
This isn't clean/ fresh.	**Das ist nicht sauber/frisch.** dahs ihst neekht <u>zow</u>•buhr/frihsh

Service is included in German restaurants and bars, as is value added tax (VAT). However, it is still typical to leave a small tip; round to the nearest euro or two for a small bill or add 5-10%, rounding to a full euro, for a larger bill. Note that it is not typical to be given a check [bill]. The server will usually just tell you your total, and you will hand the money to the server, specifying how much change you need back (so the tip is included, not left on the table later).

Paying

The check [bill], please.	**Die Rechnung, bitte.** *dee rehkh·noonk biht·tuh*
Separate checks [bills], please.	**Getrennte Rechungen, bitte.** *geh·trehn·tuh rehkh·noong·uhn biht·tuh*
It's all together.	**Alles zusammen.** *ah·luhs tsoo·zah·muhn*
Is service included?	**Ist die Bedienung im Preis enthalten?** *ihsht dee buh·dee·noonk ihm pries ehnt·hahl·tuhn*
What's this amount for?	**Wofür ist diese Summe?** *voh·fewr ihsht dee·zuh soo·muh*
I didn't have that. I had...	**Das hatte ich nicht. Ich hatte ...** *dahs hah·tuh eekh neekht eekh hah·tuh ...*
Can I...?	**Kann ich ...?** *kahn eekh ...*
pay with a credit card	**mit Kreditkarte bezahlen** *miht kreh·deet·kahr·tuh beht·sahl·uhn*
have a receipt	**eine Quittung haben** *ien·uh kvee·toonk hah·buhn*
have an itemized bill	**eine aufgeschlüsselte Rechnung haben** *ien·uh owf·guh·shlew·sehl·tuh rehkh·oong·uhn hah·buhn*
That was delicious!	**Das war lecker!** *dahs vahr leh·khehr*
I've already paid	**Ich habe schon bezahlt.** *eekh hah·buh shohn beht·sahlt*

Meals & Cooking

Breakfast

der Apfelsaft *dehr ah·pfuhl·zahft*	apple juice
der Aufschnitt *dehr owf·shniht*	cold cuts [charcuterie]
das Brot *dahs broht*	bread
das Brötchen *dahs brert·khuhn*	roll
die Butter *dee boo·tehr*	butter
das … Ei *dahs … ie*	…egg
hart/weich gekochte *hahrt/viekh guh·kohkh·tuh*	hard-/soft-boiled
der Joghurt *dehr yoh·goort*	yogurt
der Kaffee/Tee … *dehr kah·feh/tee …*	coffee/tea…
entkoffeiniert *ehnt·koh·feh·een·eert*	decaf
mit Milch *miht mihlkh*	with milk
mit Süßstoff *miht zews·shtohf*	with artificial sweetener
mit Zucker *miht tsoo·khuhr*	with sugar
schwarz *shvahrts*	black
der Käse *dehr kay·zuh*	cheese
der Kräutertee *dehr krow·tehr·tee*	herbal tea
die Marmelade *dee mahr·muh·lah·duh*	jam/jelly

Das Frühstück (breakfast) can range from a large meal, usually served buffet style, to a simple dish of bread, jam and butter. **Das Mittagessen** (lunch), typically a large and heavy meal, is normally served from 12:00 to 2:00 p.m. In larger cities, many Germans will have lunch at a beer garden or hall with cafeteria-style service. **Das Abendessen** (dinner) is served from 6:00 to 9:00 p.m. and is usually a light meal.

die Milch *dee mihlkh*	milk
der Muffin *dehr <u>moo</u>•fihn*	muffin
das Müsli *dahs <u>mew</u>•slee*	granola [muesli]
das Omelett *dahs <u>ohm</u>•luht*	omelet
der Orangensaft *dehr oh•<u>rahng</u>•uhn•zahft*	orange juice
der Pampelmusensaft	grapefruit juice
dehr pahm•puhl•<u>moo</u>•zuhn•zahft	
das Rührei *dahs <u>rew</u>•rie*	scrambled egg
der Saft *dehr zahft*	juice
der Schinken *dehr <u>shihn</u>•kuhn*	ham
das Spiegelei *dahs <u>shpeeg</u>•uh•lie*	fried egg
der Toast *dehr tohst*	toast
das Wasser *dahs <u>vah</u>•sehr*	water

Appetizers

die Appetithäppchen	finger sandwiches
dee ah•peh•<u>teet</u>•hehp•khehn	
die Aufschnittplatte *dee <u>owf</u>•shniht•plah•tuh*	cold cuts served with bread
der Bismarckhering *dehr*	marinated herring with
bees•mahrk•heh•reeng	onions
die Fleischpastete *dee <u>fliesh</u>•pah•steh•tuh*	meat pâté

die Gänseleberpastete	goose liver pâté
dee gehn·zehl·leh·behr·pah·steh·tuh	
die gefüllten Champignons	stuffed mushrooms
dee geh·fewl·tehn shahm·pee·nyohns	
der gemischte Salat *dehr geh·meesh·tuh*	mixed salad
sah·laht	
die Käseplatte *dee kay·zuh·plah·tuh*	cheese platter
das Knoblauchbrot *dahs knoh·blowkh·broht*	garlic bread
der Krabbencocktail	shrimp cocktail
dehr krahb·behn·kohk·tayl	
die russischen Eier	hard-boiled eggs with
dee roo·see·shuh ier	mayonnaise
der Räucherlachs *dehr roy·khurt·lahks*	smoked salmon
der Salat *dehr sah·laht*	salad
die Soleier *dee soh·lier*	eggs boiled in brine
der Tomatensalat	tomato salad
dehr toh·mah·tehn·sah·laht	
der Wurstsalat *dehr voorst·sah·laht*	cold cuts with onion and oil

Soup

die Backerbsensuppe	broth with crisp,
dee bahk·ehrb·sehn·zoo·puh	round noodles
die Bohnensuppe *dee boh·nuhn·zoo·puh*	bean soup
die Champignoncremesuppe	cream of mushroom
dee shahm·pee·nyohn·krehm·zoo·puh	soup
die Erbsensuppe *dee ehrb·zuhn·zoo·puh*	pea soup
die Fleischbrühe *dee fliesh·brew·uh*	bouillon
die Frittatensuppe *dee free·tah·tehn·zoo·puh*	broth with pancake strips
die Frühlingssuppe *dee frew·leeng·zoo·puh*	spring vegetable soup
die Gemüsesuppe *dee guh·mew· zuh·zoo·puh*	vegetable soup
die Gulaschsuppe *dee gool·ahsh·zoo·puh*	stewed beef in a spicy soup

die Hühnersuppe *dee hewn•ehr•zoo•puh*	chicken soup
die klare Gemüsebrühe *dee klah•ruh geh•mew•zuh•brew•uh*	vegetable broth
die Linsensuppe *dee leen•zehn•zoo•puh*	lentil soup
die Semmelknödelsuppe *dee zeh•mehl•kner•dehl•zoo•puh*	bread dumpling soup
die Tomatensuppe *dee toh•mah•tuhn•zoo•puh*	tomato soup
die Zwiebelsuppe *dee tsvee•behl•zoo•puh*	onion soup

Fish & Seafood

der Aal *dehr ahl*	eel
die Auster *dee ow•stehr*	oyster
die Brachse *dee brahk•suh*	bream
der Barsch *dehr bahrsh*	perch
der Brathering *dehr brah•theh•reeng*	fried sour herring
der Dorsch *dehr dohrsh*	cod
die Forelle *dee foh•reh•luh*	trout
die Garnele *dee gahr•neh•luh*	shrimp
der Heilbutt *dehr hiel•boot*	halibut
der Hering *dehr heh•rihng*	herring
der Hummer *dehr hoo•mehr*	lobster
der Krebs *dehr krehbs*	crab
der Lachs *dehr lahks*	salmon
die Makrele *dee mah•kreh•luh*	mackerel
die Muschel *dee moo•shuhl*	clam
der Oktopus *dehr ohk•toh•poos*	octopus
die Sardelle *dee sahr•deh•luh*	anchovy
die Sardine *dee zahr•dee•nuh*	sardine
die Scholle *dee shoh•luh*	flounder
der Schwertfisch *dehr shvehrt•fihsh*	swordfish
der Seebarsch *dehr zeh•bahrsh*	sea bass

die Seezunge *dee <u>zeh</u>·tsoong·uh*	sole
der Tintenfisch *dehr <u>tihn</u>·tuhn·fihsh*	squid
der Thunfisch *dehr <u>toon</u>·fihsh*	tuna

Meat & Poultry

die Berliner Buletten *dee behr·<u>lee</u>·nuh boo·<u>leh</u>·tehn*	fried meatballs, a specialty of Berlin
der Braten *dehr <u>brah</u>·tuhn*	roast
die Bratwurst *dee <u>braht</u>·voorst*	fried sausage
die Ente *dee <u>ehn</u>·tuh*	duck
das Filet *dahs <u>fee</u>·leh*	filet
der Fleischkäse *dehr <u>fliesh</u>·kay·zuh*	a kind of meatloaf
die Frikadelle *dee free·kah·<u>dehl</u>·luh*	fried meatballs
das Gulasch *dahs <u>gool</u>·ahsh*	stewed beef with spicy paprika gravy
der Hackbraten *dehr <u>hahk</u>·brah·tuhn*	meatloaf
das Hackfleisch *dahs <u>hahk</u>·fliesh*	ground meat
das Hühnchen *dahs <u>hewn</u>·khuhn*	chicken
das Spanferkel *dahs <u>shpahn</u>·fehr·kehl*	crunchy roasted suckling pig
das Kalbfleisch *dahs <u>kahlb</u>·fliesh*	veal
das Kaninchen *dahs kah·<u>nihn</u>·khehn*	rabbit

das Kotelett *dahs koht·leht*	pork chop
das Lamm *dahs lahm*	lamb
die Leber *dee leh·behr*	liver
die Niere *dee nee·ruh*	kidney
das Pökelfleisch *dahs pehr·kehl·fliesh*	pickled meat
der Rinderbraten *dehr reen·dehr·brah·tuhn*	roast beef
das Rindfleisch *dahs rihnt·fliesh*	beef
die Rouladen *dee roo·lah·dehn*	stuffed beef slices, rolled and braised in brown gravy
der Sauerbraten *dehr zow·ehr·brah·tuhn*	beef roast, marinated with herbs, in a rich sauce
der Schinken *dehr shihn·kuhn*	ham
der Schinkenspeck *dehr shihn·kuhn·shpehk*	bacon
das Schmorfleisch *dahs shmohr·fliesh*	stewed meat
das Schweinefleisch *dahs shvien·uh·fliesh*	pork
der Schweinebraten *dehr shvien·brah·tuhn*	roast pork
das Steak *dahs shtayhk*	steak
der Tafelspitz *dehr tah·fehl·shpeets*	Viennese-style boiled beef
der Truthahn *dehr troot·hahn*	turkey
das Wiener Schnitzel *dahs viee·nehr shniht·tzehl*	veal cutlet

die Wurst *dee voorst*	sausage
die Zunge *dee tsoong·uh*	tongue

Vegetables & Staples

die Artischocke *dee ahr·tee·shoh·kuh*	artichoke
die Aubergine *dee ow·behr·gee·neh*	eggplant [aubergine]
die Avocado *dee ah·voh·kah·doh*	avocado
die Bohnen *dee boh·nuhn*	beans
die grünen Bohnen *dee grew·nuhn boh·nuhn*	green beans
der Blumenkohl *dehr bloo·muhn·kohl*	cauliflower
der Brokkoli *dehr broh·koh·lee*	broccoli
die Erbse *dee ehrb·zuh*	pea
das gemischte Gemüse *dahs geh·meesh·tuh geh·mew·zuh*	mixed vegetables
das Gemüse *dahs geh·mew·zuh*	vegetable
die Gurke *dee goor·kuh*	cucumber
die Kartoffel *dee kahr·toh·fuhl*	potato
der Kartoffelbrei *dehr kahr·toh·fehl·brie*	mashed potato
der Knoblauch *dehr knoh·blowkh*	garlic
der Kohl *dehr kohl*	cabbage
der Krautsalat *dehr krowt·sah·laht*	coleslaw
der Mais *dehr mies*	corn
der Maiskolben *dehr mies·kohl·behn*	corn on the cob
die Möhre *dee mer·ruh*	carrot
die Olive *dee oh·lee·vuh*	olive
der rote/grüne Paprika *dehr roh·teh/grew·neh pah·pree·kuh*	red/green pepper
die Pasta *dee pah·stah*	pasta
die Pellkartoffeln *dee pehl·kahr·toh·fehl·ehn*	boiled, unpeeled potatoes

der Pilz *dehr pihlts* — mushroom
der Reis *dehr ries* — rice
der Rettich *dehr reh•teekh* — radish
das Roggenbrot *dahs roh•gehn•broht* — rye bread
der Salat *dehr sah•laht* — lettuce
der Spargel *dehr shpahr•gehl* — asparagus
der Spinat *dehr shpee•naht* — spinach
die Tomate *dee toh•mah•teh* — tomato
die Zucchini *dee tsoo•khee•nee* — zucchini [courgette]
die Zwiebel *dee tsvee•buhl* — onion

Fruit

die Ananas *dee ah•nah•nahs* — pineapple
der Apfel *dehr ahp•fuhl* — apple
die Apfelsine *dee ah•pfehl•zee•nuh* — orange
die Banane *dee bah•nah•nuh* — banana
die Birne *dee beer•nuh* — pear
die Blaubeere *dee blow•beh•ruh* — blueberry
die Erdbeere *dee ehrd•beh•ruh* — strawberry
die Himbeere *dee hihm•beh•ruh* — raspberry
die Kirsche *dee keer•shuh* — cherry

die Limette *dee lee·meh·tuh*	lime
die Melone *dee meh·loh·nuh*	melon
das Obst *dahs ohpst*	fruit
die Pampelmuse *dee pahm·pehl·moo·zuh*	grapefruit
der Pfirsich *dehr pfeer·zeekh*	peach
die Pflaume *dee pflow·muh*	plum
die rote/schwarze Johannisbeere	red/black currant
dee roh·tuh/shvahr·tsuh yoh·hah·nihs·beh·ruh	
die Weintraube *dee vien·trow·buh*	grape
die Zitrone *dee tsee·troh·nuh*	lemon

Cheese

der Appenzeller *dehr ah·pehn·tseh·lehr*	hard cheese from Switzerland
der Blauschimmelkäse	blue cheese
dehr blow·shihm·mehl·kay·zuh	
der Emmentaler *dehr ehm·mehn·tah·lehr*	mild Swiss cheese
der Frischkäse *dehr freesh·kay·zuh*	cream cheese
der Handkäse *dehr hahnt·kay·zuh*	sharp, soft cheese
die Käseplatte *dee kay·zuh·plah·tuh*	cheese platter
der Schafskäse *dehr shahf·kay·zuh*	feta cheese
der Tilsiter *dehr teel·seet·ehr*	semi-soft Austrian cheese
der Ziegenkäse *dehr tsee·guhn·kay·zuh*	goat cheese

Dessert

der Apfelkuchen *dehr ah·pfuhl·kookh·uhn*	apple pie or tart
das Eis *dahs ies*	ice cream
der Käsekuchen *dehr kay·zuh·kookh·uhn*	cheesecake
der Krapfen *dehr krah·pfehn*	fritter
die Makrone *dee mah·kroh·nuh*	macaroon
das Marzipan *dahs mahr·tsee·pahn*	marzipan
der Obstsalat *dehr ohpst·sah·laht*	fruit salad

die Rote Grütze *dee roh·tuh grewt·zuh* — berry pudding

die Schwarzwälder Kirschtorte — Black Forest chocolate
dee schvahrts·vahl·dehr keersh·tohr·tuh — cake with cherries

die Torte *dee tohr·tuh* — cake

Sauces & Condiments

salt	**salz** *sahlts*	
pepper	**pfeffer** *pfehf·fehr*	
mustard	**senf** *sehnf*	
ketchup	**ketchup** *ket·shahp*	

At the Market

Where are the trolleys/baskets?	**Wo sind die Einkaufswagen/Einkaufskörbe?** *voh zihnt dee ien·kowfs·vah·guhn/ien·kowfs·kehr·buh*
Where is…?	**Wo ist …?** *voh ihsht …*
I'd like some of that/this.	**Ich möchte etwas von dem/diesem.** *eekh merkh·tuh eht·vahs fohn dehm/dee·zuhm*
Can I taste it?	**Kann ich es kosten?** *kahn eekh ehs kohs·tuhn*
I'd like…	**Ich möchte …** *eekh merkh·tuh …*
a kilo/half-kilo of…	**ein Kilo/halbes Kilo …** *ien kee·loh/ hahl·buhs kee·loh …*
a liter of…	**einen Liter …** *ien·uhn lee·tehr …*
a piece of…	**ein Stück …** *ien shtewk …*
a slice of…	**eine Scheibe …** *ien·uh shie·buh …*
More/less	**Mehr/Weniger** *mehr/veh·nee·guhr*

Local markets that sell fresh produce and homemade goods can be found in most cities throughout Germany. The days and hours of operation vary widely. Your hotel concierge or a tourist information office can provide details.

YOU MAY HEAR...

Kann ich Ihnen helfen? *kahn eekh eehn•uhn hehl•fuhn*		Can I help you?
Was möchten Sie? *vahs merkh•tuhn zee*		What would you like?
Noch etwas? *nohkh eht•vahs*		Anything else?
Das macht ... Euro. *dahs mahkht ... oy•roh*		That's...euros.

How much?	**Wie viel kostet das?** *vee feel kohs•tuht dahs*
Where do I pay?	**Wo bezahle ich?** *voh beht•sahl•uh eekh*
A bag, please.	**Eine Tüte, bitte.** *ien•uh tew•tuh biht•tuh*
I'm being helped.	**Ich werde schon bedient.** *eekh vehr•duh shohn buh•deent*

For Conversion Tables, see page 171.

For Meals & Cooking, see page 67.

In the Kitchen

bottle opener	**der Flaschenöffner** *dehr flah•shuhn•erf•nehr*	
bowl	**die Schüssel** *dee shew•suhl*	
can opener	**der Dosenöffner** *dehr doh•zuhn•erf•nuhr*	
corkscrew	**der Korkenzieher** *dehr kohr•kuhn•tsee•uhr*	
cup	**die Tasse** *dee tah•suh*	
fork	**die Gabel** *dee gah•buhl*	
frying pan	**die Bratpfanne** *dee braht•pfah•nuh*	
glass	**das Glas** *dahs glahs*	
(steak) knife	**das (Steak-) Messer** *dahs (shtehk•) meh•sehr*	
measuring cup	**der Messbecher** *dehr mehs•beh•khuhr*	
measuring spoon	**der Messlöffel** *dehr mehs•ler•fuhl*	
napkin	**die Serviette** *dee sehr•vyeh•tuh*	
plate	**der Teller** *dehr teh•lehr*	

YOU MAY SEE...

MINDESTENS HALTBAR BIS ...	best before...
KALORIEN	calories
FETTARM	low fat
GEKÜHLT LAGERN	keep refrigerated
KANN SPUREN VON ... BEINHALTEN	may contain traces of...
MIKROWELLENGEEIGNET	microwaveable
FÜR VEGETARIER GEEIGNET	suitable for vegetarians

pot	**der Topf** *dehr tohpf*
spatula	**der Spatel** *dehr shpah•tuhl*
spoon	**der Löffel** *dehr ler•fuhl*

Measurements in Europe are metric – and that applies to the weight of food too. If you tend to think in pounds and ounces, it's worth brushing up on what the metric equivalent is before you go shopping for fruit and veg in markets and supermarkets. Five hundred grams, or half a kilo, is a common quantity to order, and that converts to just over a pound (17.65 ounces, to be precise).

Drinks

ESSENTIAL

The wine list/drink menu, please.	**Die Weinkarte/Getränkekarte, bitte.** *dee vien·kahr·tuh/geh·trehnk·uh·kahr·tuh biht·tuh*
What do you recommend?	**Was empfehlen Sie?** *vahs ehm·pfeh·luhn zee*
I'd like a bottle/ glass of red/ white wine.	**Ich möchte gern eine Flasche/ein Glas Rotwein/Weißwein.** *eekh merkh·tuh gehrn ien·uh flah·shuh/ien glahs roht·vien/vies·vien*
The house wine, please.	**Den Hauswein, bitte.** *dehn hows·vien biht·tuh*
Another bottle/glass, please.	**Noch eine Flasche/ein Glas, bitte.** *nohkh ien·uh flah·shuh/ien glahs biht·tuh*
I'd like a local beer.	**Ich möchte gern ein Bier aus der Region.** *eekh merkh·tuh gehrn ien beer ows dehr rehg·yohn*
Can I buy you a drink?	**Darf ich Ihnen einen ausgeben?** *dahrf eekh eehn·uhn ows·geh·buhn*
Cheers!	**Prost!** *prohst*

A coffee/tea, please.	**Einen Kaffee/Tee, bitte.**
	ien•uhn kah•feh/tee biht•tuh
Black.	**Schwarz.** *shvahrts*
With…	**Mit …** *miht …*
milk	**Milch** *mihlkh*
sugar	**Zucker** *tsoo•kehr*
artificial sweetener	**Süßstoff** *zews•shtohf*
…, please.	**…, bitte.** *…, biht•tuh*
A juice	**Einen Saft** *ien•uhn zahft*
A soda	**Eine Cola** *ien•uh koh•lah*
A still/sparkling water	**Ein stilles Wasser/Wasser mit Kohlensäure** *ien shtihl•uhs vah•sehr/ vah•sehr miht kohl•ehn•zoy•ruh*

Non-alcoholic Drinks

die Cola *dee koh•lah*	soda
der Kaffee *dehr kah•feh*	coffee
der Kakao *dehr kah•kah•ow*	hot chocolate
die Milch *dee mihlkh*	milk
der Saft *dehr zahft*	juice
der (Eis-)Tee *dehr (ies) tee*	(iced) tea
das stille Wasser/Wasser mit Kohlensäure *dahs shtihl•uh vah•sehr/ vah•sehr miht kohl•ehn•zoy•ruh*	still/sparkling water

YOU MAY HEAR...

Möchten Sie etwas trinken? *merkh·tuhn zee eht·vahs trihn·kuhn*

Can I get you a drink?

Mit Milch oder Zucker? *miht mihelkh oh·dehr tsoo·kehr*

With milk or sugar?

Stilles Wasser oder mit Kohlensäure? *shtihl·uhs vah·sehr oh·dehr miht koh·lehn·zoy·ruh*

Still or sparkling water?

Aperitifs, Cocktails & Liqueurs

der Gin *dehr djihn*	gin
der Rum *dehr room*	rum
der Scotch *dehr skohch*	scotch
der Tequila *dehr teh·kee·lah*	tequila
der Weinbrand *dehr vien·brahnt*	brandy
der Whisky *dehr vees·kee*	whisky
der Wodka *dehr voht·kah*	vodka

Kaffee (coffee) is popular in Germany and a fresh cup can be found at a **Café** or **Kaffeehaus**. **Kräutertee** (herbal tea) is another common beverage, and pharmacies, supermarkets and health-food stores carry a variety of teas.

Beer

das Flaschenbier *dahs <u>flah</u>·shuhn·beer*	bottled beer
das Bier vom Fass *dahs beer fohm fahs*	draft beer
das Helle/Pilsner *dahs <u>heh</u>·luh/<u>pihls</u>·nehr*	lager/pilsner
die Halbe *dee <u>hahlb</u>·uh*	pint
das ... Bier *dahs ... beer*	...beer
dunkle/helle <u>*doon*</u>·*kluh/<u>heh</u>·luh*	dark/light
regionale/importierte	local/imported
reh·gyoh·<u>nah</u>·luh/eem·pohr·<u>teer</u>·tuh	
alkoholfreie *ahl·koh·hohl·<u>frie</u>·uh*	non-alcoholic

There are more than 1,000 breweries in Germany, producing more than 5,000 different brands of beer.
Styles include: **Altbier** (high hops content, similar to British ale), **Bockbier** (high malt content), **Hefeweizen** (pale, made from wheat), **Kölsch** (lager, brewed in Cologne), **Malzbier** (dark and sweet) and **Pilsener** (pale and strong). Popular German brands include: **Augustiner™**, **Beck's™**, **Jever™**, **Löwenbräu™** and **Spaten™**.

Wine

der Champagner *dehr shahm·pahn·yehr*	champagne
der Wein *dehr vien*	wine
der Dessertwein *dehr deh·sehrt·vien*	dessert wine
der Hauswein/Tischwein	house/table wine
dehr hows·vien/tihsh·vien	
der Rotwein/Weißwein	red/white wine
dehr roht·vien/vies·vien	
der trockene/liebliche Wein	dry/sweet wine
dehr troh·keh·neh/lee·blee·kheh vien	
der Schaumwein *dehr showm·vien*	sparkling wine

On the Menu

der Aal *dehr ahl*	eel
die Ananas *dee ahn·ah·nahs*	pineapple
der Aperitif *dehr ah·pehr·ee·teef*	aperitif
der Apfel *dehr ahp·fehl*	apple
die Apfelsine *dee ah·pfuhl·zee·nuh*	orange
der Apfelwein *dehr ah·pfuhl·vien*	cider (alcoholic)
die Aprikose *dee ah·pree·koh·zuh*	apricot
die Artischocke *dee ahr·tee·shoh·kuh*	artichoke
die Aubergine *dee ow·behr·gee·nuh*	eggplant [aubergine]
der Aufschnitt *dehr owf·shniht*	cold cuts [charcuterie]
die Auster *dee ows·tuhr*	oyster
die Avocado *dee ah·voh·kah·doh*	avocado
die Backpflaume *dee bahk·pflow·muh*	prune
der Bacon *dehr bah·kohn*	bacon
die Banane *dee bah·nah·nuh*	banana
der Barsch *dehr bahrsh*	bass

das Basilikum *dahs bah-zee-lee-koom*	basil
das Bier *dahs beer*	beer
die Birne *dee beer-nuh*	pear
die Blaubeere *dee blow-beh-ruh*	blueberry
der Blauschimmelkäse *dehr blow-shihm-mehl-kay-zuh*	blue cheese
der Blumenkohl *dehr bloo-muhn-kohl*	cauliflower
die Blutwurst *dee bloot-voorst*	blood sausage
die Bohne *dee boh-nuh*	bean
die Bouillon *dee boo-yohn*	broth
der Branntwein *dehr brahnt-vien*	brandy
der Braten *dehr brah-tuhn*	roast
die Brombeere *dee brohm-beh-ruh*	blackberry
das Brot *dahs broht*	bread
das Brötchen *dahs brert-khehn*	roll
die Brunnenkresse *dee broo-nuhn-kreh-zuh*	watercress
die (Hühnchen-) Brust *dee (hewn-khehn-) broost*	breast (of chicken)
die Butter *dee boo-tehr*	butter
die Buttermilch *dee boo-tehr-mihlkh*	buttermilk
die Cashewnuss *dee keh-shoo-noos*	cashew
der Chikorée *dehr chee-koh-reh*	chicory
die Chilischote *dee chee-lee-shoh-tuh*	chili pepper
die Cola *dee koh-lah*	soda
der Cracker *dehr kreh-kehr*	cracker
die Datteln *dee dah-tuhln*	dates
der Dessertwein *dehr deh-zehrt-vien*	dessert wine
der Dill *dehr dihl*	dill
der Donut *dehr doh-nuht*	doughnut
der Dorsch *dehr dohrsh*	cod

BAUERNSCHE...

Erdbeeren
aus eigenem Anbau

das Ei *dahs ie*	egg
das Eigelb *dahs ie•gehlb*	egg yolk
der Eierkuchen *dehr ier•koo•khuhn*	pancake
das Eis *dahs ies*	ice cream
der Eiswürfel *dehr ies•vewr•fehl*	ice (cube)
das Eiweiß *dahs ie•vies*	egg white
die Endivie *dee ehn•dee•vee•uh*	endive
die Ente *dee ehn•tuh*	duck
die Erbsen *dee ehrb•zuhn*	peas
die Erdbeere *dee ehrd•beh•ruh*	strawberry
die Erdnuss *dee ehrd•noos*	peanut
der Essig *dehr eh•zeek*	vinegar
das Estragon *dahs eh•strah•gohn*	tarragon
der Fasan *dehr fah•zahn*	pheasant
die Feige *dee fie•guh*	fig
der Fenchel *dehr fehn•khehl*	fennel
der Fisch *dehr fihsh*	fish
das Fleisch *dahs fliesh*	meat
die Fleischstücke *dee fliesh•shtew•kuh*	chopped meat
die Forelle *dee foh•reh•luh*	trout
die Gans *dee gahns*	goose

die Gänseleberpastete	goose liver pâté
dee gehn·zehl·leh·behr·pah·steh·tuh	
die Garnele *dee gahr·neh·luh*	shrimp
das Gebäck *dahs guh·behk*	pastry
das Geflügel *dahs guh·flew·gehl*	poultry
das Gemüse *dahs geh·mew·zuh*	vegetable
die Gewürze *dee guh·vewr·tsuh*	spices
die Gewürzgurke *dee guh·vewrts·goor·kuh*	pickle/gherkin
der Gin *dehr djihn*	gin
der Granatapfel *dehr grah·naht·ahp·fehl*	pomegranate
die grünen Bohnen *dee grew·nuhn boh·nuhn*	green beans
die Guave *dee gwah·veh*	guava
die Gurke *dee goor·kuh*	cucumber
die Hachse *dee hahk·suh*	shank
der Hamburger *dehr hahm·boor·gehr*	hamburger
der Hammel *dehr hah·mehl*	mutton
die Haselnuss *dee hah·zuhl·noos*	hazelnut
der Heilbutt *dehr hiel·boot*	halibut
die Henne *dee heh·nuh*	hen
der Hering *dehr heh·reeng*	herring
das Herz *dahs hehrts*	heart
die Himbeere *dee heem·beh·ruh*	raspberry
der Honig *dehr hoh·neek*	honey
der Hotdog *dehr hoht·dohg*	hot dog
das Hühnchen *dahs hewn·khehn*	chicken
der Hummer *dehr hoo·mehr*	lobster
der Hüttenkäse *dehr hew·tuhn·kay·zuh*	cottage cheese
der Imbiss *dehr ihm·buhs*	snack
der Ingwer *dehr eeng·vehr*	ginger
die Innereien *dee ihn·eh·rie·uhn*	organ meat [offal]
der Joghurt *dehr yoh·goort*	yogurt

der Kaffee *dehr kah·feh*	coffee
das Kalb *dahs kahlb*	veal
das Kaninchen *dahs kah·neen·khehn*	rabbit
die Kaper *dee kah·pehr*	caper
das Karamell *dahs kah·rah·mehl*	caramel
die Kartoffel *dee kahr·toh·fehl*	potato
die Kartoffelchips *dee kahr·toh·fehl·cheeps*	potato chips [crisps]
der Käse *dehr kay·zuh*	cheese
die Kastanie *dee kah·stahn·yuh*	chestnut
der Keks *dehr keks*	cookie [biscuit]
der Kerbel *dehr kehr·behl*	chervil
der Ketchup *dehr keh·chuhp*	ketchup
die Kichererbse *dee kee·khehr·ehrb·zuh*	chickpea
die Kirsche *dee keer·shuh*	cherry
die Kiwi *dee kee·vee*	kiwi
der Kloß *dehr klohs*	dumpling
der Knoblauch *dehr knoh·blowkh*	garlic
die Koblauchsauce *dee knoh·blowkh·zow·suh*	garlic sauce
der Kohl *dehr kohl*	cabbage
die Kokosnuss *dee koh·kohs·noos*	coconut
das Kompott *dahs kohm·poht*	stewed fruit
die Konfitüre *dee kohn·fee·tew·ruh*	jelly
der Koriander *dehr koh·ree·ahn·dehr*	cilantro [coriander]
die Kräuter *dee kroyt·uhr*	herbs
die Kraftbrühe *dee krahft·brew·uh*	consommé
der Krebs *dehr krehbs*	crab
das Krustentier *dahs kroos·tehn·tyehr*	shellfish
der Kuchen *dehr kookh·uhn*	pie
der Kümmel *dehr kew·mehl*	caraway
der Kürbis *dehr kewr·bees*	squash
die Kutteln *dee koo·tehln*	tripe

der Lachs *dehr lahks*	salmon
das Lamm *dahs lahm*	lamb
die Lauchzwiebel *dee <u>lowkh</u>•svee•buhl*	scallion [spring onion]
die Leber *dee <u>leh</u>•buhr*	liver
die Lende *dee <u>lehn</u>•duh*	loin
das Lendenfilet *dahs lehn•dehn•<u>fee</u>•leh*	sirloin
der Likör *dehr lee•<u>ker</u>*	liqueur
die Limette *dee lee•<u>meh</u>•tuh*	lime
die Limonade *dee lee•moh•<u>nah</u>•duh*	lemonade
die Linse *dee <u>leen</u>•zuh*	lentil
das Loorbeerblatt *dahs <u>lohr</u>•behr•blaht*	bay leaf
der Mais *dehr mies*	sweet corn
das Maismehl *dahs <u>mies</u>•mehl*	cornmeal
die Makkaroni *dee mah•kah•<u>roh</u>•nee*	macaroni
die Makrele *dee mah•<u>krehl</u>•uh*	mackerel
die Mandarine *dee mahn•dah•<u>reen</u>•uh*	tangerine
die Mandel *dee <u>mahn</u>•duhl*	almond
die Mango *dee <u>mahn</u>•goh*	mango
die Margarine *dee mahr•guh•<u>ree</u>•nuh*	margarine
die Marmelade *dee mahr•muh•<u>lah</u>•duh*	marmalade/jam
das Marzipan *dahs <u>mahr</u>•tsee•pahn*	marzipan

die Mayonnaise *dee mah·yoh·nay·zuh*	mayonnaise
die Meerbarbe *dee mehr·bahr·buh*	red mullet
die Meeresfrüchte *dee meh·rehs·frewkh·tuh*	seafood
die Melone *dee meh·loh·nuh*	melon
die Milch *dee mihlkh*	milk
das Milchmixgetränk *dahs mihlkh·mihks·geh·traynk*	milk shake
die Minze *dee mihn·tsuh*	mint
die Möhre *dee mer·ruh*	carrot
die Muschel *dee moo·shehl*	clam
der Muskat *dehr moos·kaht*	nutmeg
die Nelke *dee nehl·kuh*	clove
die Niere *dee nee·ruh*	kidney
die Nudel *dee noo·dehl*	noodle
der Nugat *dehr noo·gaht*	nougat
die Nüsse *dee new·suh*	nuts
das Obst *dahs ohbst*	fruit
der Ochse *dehr ohkh·suh*	ox
der Ochsenschwanz *dehr ohk·sehn·shvahnts*	oxtail
der Oktopus *dehr ohk·toh·poos*	octopus
die Olive *dee oh·lee·veh*	olive
das Olivenöl *dahs oh·lee·vehn·erl*	olive oil
das Omelett *dahs ohm·leht*	omelet
der Orangenlikör *dehr oh·rahn·jehn·lee·ker*	orange liqueur
das Oregano *dahs oh·reh·gah·noh*	oregano
die Pampelmuse *dee pahm·puhl·moo·zuh*	grapefruit
der Pansen *dehr pahn·sehn*	tripe
die Papaya *dee pah·pah·yah*	papaya
der Paprika *dehr pah·pree·kuh*	paprika
die Paprikaschote *dee pah·pree·kah·shoh·tuh*	pepper (vegetable)
die Pastinake *dee pah·stee·nahk·uh*	parsnip

die Pekannuss *dee peh-kahn-noos*	pecan
das Perlhuhn *dahs pehrl-hoon*	guinea fowl
die Petersilie *dee peh-tehr-see-lee-uh*	parsley
der Pfannkuchen *dehr pfahn-koo-khuhn*	pancake
der Pfeffer *dehr pfeh-fehr*	pepper (seasoning)
der Pfirsich *dehr pfeer-zeekh*	peach
die Pflaume *dee pflow-muh*	plum
der Pilz *dehr pihlts*	mushroom
die Pizza *dee pee-tsah*	pizza
die Pommes frites *dee pohm freets*	French fries
der Porree *dehr poh-reh*	leek
der Portwein *dehr pohrt-vien*	port
die Preiselbeere *dee prie-zuhl-beh-ruh*	cranberry
der Rahmkäse *dehr rahm-kay-zuh*	cream cheese
der Reis *dehr ries*	rice
der Rettich *dehr reh-teekh*	radish
der Rhabarber *dehr rah-bahr-behr*	rhubarb
der Rinderbraten *dehr reen-dehr-brah-tuhn*	roast beef
das Rindfleisch *dahs rihnt-fliesh*	beef
der Rosenkohl *dehr roh-zuhn-kohl*	Brussels sprouts
die Rosine *dee roh-zee-nuh*	raisin
der Rosmarin *dehr rohs-mah-reen*	rosemary
die rote Johannisbeere *dee roh-tuh yoh-hah-nihs-beh-ruh*	red currant
der Rotkohl *dehr roht-kohl*	red cabbage
die Rübe *dee rew-beh*	beet/turnip
der Rum *dehr room*	rum
der Safran *dehr zahf-rahn*	saffron
der Saft *dehr zahft*	juice
die Sahne *dee zah-nuh*	cream
die Salami *dee zah-lah-mee*	salami

der Salat *dehr sah•laht*	lettuce/salad
der Salbei *dehr zahl•bie*	sage
das Salz *dahs zahlts*	salt
das Sandwich *dahs sahnd•weetsh*	sandwich
die Sardelle *dee sahr•dehl•uh*	anchovy
die Sardine *dee zahr•dee•nuh*	sardine
die Sauce *dee zows•uh*	sauce
die Sauerkirsche *dee zow•ehr•keer•shuh*	sour cherry
die saure Sahne *dee zow•ruh zah•nuh*	sour cream
die Schalotte *dee shah•loh•tuh*	shallot
die scharfe Pfeffersauce *dee shahr•fuh pfeh•fehr•zow•suh*	hot pepper sauce
das Schaumgebäck *dahs showm•guh•behk*	meringue
der Schellfisch *dehr shehl•fihsh*	haddock
der Schinken *dehr sheen•kuhn*	ham
die Schlagsahne *dee shlahg•zah•nuh*	whipped cream
die Schnecke *dee shnehkh•uh*	snail
der Schnittlauch *dehr shniht•lowkh*	chives
das Schnitzel *dahs shniht•tzuhl*	chop
die Schokolade *dee shoh•koh•lah•duh*	chocolate
die Schulter *dee shool•tehr*	shoulder
die schwarze Johannisbeere *dee shvahr•tsuh yoh•hah•nees•beh•ruh*	black currant
das Schweinefleisch *dahs shvien•uh•fliesh*	pork
der Schwertfisch *dehr shvehrt•fihsh*	swordfish
der Scotch *dehr skohtsh*	scotch
der Seebarsch *dehr zeh•bahrsh*	sea bass
der Seehecht *dehr zeh•hehkht*	hake
der Seeteufel *dehr zeh•toy•fuhl*	monkfish
die Seezunge *dee zeh•tsoong•uh*	sole
der Sellerie *dehr zeh•luh•ree*	celery

der Senf *dehr zehnf*	mustard
der Sherry *dehr <u>shehr</u>•ee*	sherry
der Sirup *dehr <u>zew</u>•roop*	syrup
das Soda-Wasser *dahs soh•dah•<u>vah</u>•sehr*	soda water
die Sojabohne *dee <u>zoh</u>•yah•boh•nuh*	soybean [soya bean]
die Sojamilch *dee <u>zoh</u>•yah•mihlkh*	soymilk [soya milk]
die Sojasauce *dee <u>zoh</u>•yah•zow•suh*	soy sauce
die Sojasprossen *dee <u>soh</u>•jah•shproh•suhn*	bean sprouts
die Spaghetti *dee shpah•<u>geh</u>•tee*	spaghetti
das Spanferkel *dahs <u>shpahn</u>•fehr•kehl*	crunchy roasted suckling pig
der Spargel *dehr <u>shpahr</u>•gehl*	asparagus
der Spinat *dehr shpee•<u>naht</u>*	spinach
die Spirituosen *dee shpee•ree•<u>twoh</u>•zuhn*	spirits
die Stachelbeere *dee <u>shtah</u>•khehl•beh•ruh*	gooseberry
das Steak *dahs stehk*	steak
die Suppe *dee <u>zoo</u>•puh*	soup
die Süßigkeiten *dee <u>zew</u>•seekh•kie•tuhn*	candy [sweets]
die Süßkartoffel *dee <u>zews</u>•kahr•toh•fuhl*	sweet potato
die süßsaure Sauce *dee <u>zews</u>•zow•ruh zow•suh*	sweet and sour sauce
der Süßstoff *dehr <u>zews</u>•shtohf*	sweetener
der Tee *dehr teh*	tea
der Thunfisch *dehr <u>toon</u>•fihsh*	tuna
der Thymian *dehr <u>tew</u>•mee•ahn*	thyme
der Tintenfisch *dehr <u>teen</u>•tuhn•fihsh*	squid
der Toast *dehr tohst*	toast
das Tofu *dahs <u>toh</u>•foo*	tofu
die Tomate *dee <u>toh</u>•mah•tuh*	tomato
das Tonic *dahs <u>toh</u>•neek*	tonic water
die Trüffel *dee <u>trew</u>•fuhl*	truffles
der Truthahn *dehr <u>troot</u>•hahn*	turkey

die Vanille *dee vah•nee•luh*	vanilla
die Wachtel *dee vahkh•tehl*	quail
die Waffel *dee vah•fuhl*	waffle
die Walnuss *dee vahl•noos*	walnut
das Wasser *dahs vah•sehr*	water
die Wassermelone *dee vah•sehr•meh•loh•nuh*	watermelon
der Wein *dehr vien*	wine
die Weintrauben *dee vien•trow•buhn*	grapes
der Weizen *dehr vie•tsuhn*	wheat
der Wermut *dehr vehr•moot*	vermouth
der Whisky *dehr vees•kee*	whisky
das Wild *dahs vihlt*	game/venison
der Wodka *dehr vohd•kah*	vodka
die Wurst *dee voorst*	sausage
der Zackenbarsch *dehr tsah•kehn•bahrsh*	sea perch
das Zicklein *dahs tsihk•lien*	kid (young goat)
die Ziege *dee tsee•guh*	goat
der Ziegenkäse *dehr tsee•guhn•kay•zuh*	goat cheese
der Zimt *dehr tsihmt*	cinnamon
die Zitrone *dee tsee•troh•nuh*	lemon
die Zucchini *dee tsoo•kee•nee*	zucchini [courgette]
der Zucker *dehr tsoo•kehr*	sugar
die Zunge *dee tsoong•uh*	tongue
die Zwiebel *dee tsvee•buhl*	onion

People

Conversation   95

Romance   101

Conversation

ESSENTIAL

Hello!	**Hallo!** *hah·loh*
How are you?	**Wie geht es Ihnen?** *vee geht ehs eehn·uhn*
Fine, thanks.	**Gut, danke.** *goot dahn·kuh*
Excuse me!	**Entschuldigung!** *ehnt·shool·dee·goong*
Do you speak English?	**Sprechen Sie Englisch?** *shpreh·khuhn zee ehn·gleesh*
What's your name?	**Wie heißen Sie?** *vee hie·suhn zee*
My name is…	**Mein Name ist …** *mien nahm·uh ihst …*
Nice to meet you.	**Schön, Sie kennenzulernen.** *shern zee keh·nehn·tsoo·lehr·nehn*
Where are you from?	**Woher kommen Sie?** *voh·hehr koh·muhn zee*
I'm from the U.S./U.K.	**Ich komme aus den USA/Großbritannien.** *eekh koh·muh ows dehn oo·ehs·ah/ grohs·bree·tah·nee·ehn*
What do you do for a living?	**Was machen Sie beruflich?** *vahs mah·khuhn zee beh·roof·likh*
I work for…	**Ich arbeite für …** *eekh ahr·bie·tuh fewr …*
I'm a student.	**Ich bin Student.** *eekh bihn shtoo·dehnt*
I'm retired.	**Ich bin Rentner.** *eekh been rehnt·nehr*
Do you like…?	**Mögen Sie …?** *mer·guhn zee …*
Goodbye.	**Auf Wiedersehen.** *owf vee·dehr·zehn*
See you later.	**Bis bald.** *bihs bahld*

95

When addressing anyone but a very close friend, it is polite to use a title: **Herr** (Mr.), **Frau** (Miss/Ms./Mrs.) or **Herr Dr.** (Dr.), and to speak to him or her using **Sie**, the formal form of 'you', until you are asked to use the familiar **Du**.

Language Difficulties

Do you speak English?	**Sprechen Sie Englisch?** *shpreh*•khehn zee ehn•gleesh
Does anyone here speak English?	**Spricht hier jemand Englisch?** shpreekht heer yeh•mahnt ehn•gleesh
I don't speak (much) German.	**Ich spreche kein (nicht viel) Deutsch.** eekh shpreh•khuh kien (neekht feel) doych
Can you speak more slowly, please?	**Können Sie bitte langsamer sprechen?** ker•nuhn zee biht•tuh lahng•sahm•ehr shpreh•khuhn
Can you repeat that, please?	**Können Sie das bitte wiederholen?** ker•nuhn zee dahs biht•tuh vee•dehr•hoh•luhn
Excuse me?	**Wie bitte?** vee biht•tuh
What was that?	**Was haben Sie gesagt?** vahs hah•buhn zee guh•zahg
Can you spell it?	**Können Sie das buchstabieren?** ker•nuhn zee dahs book•shtah•bee•ruhn

YOU MAY HEAR…

Ich spreche nur wenig Englisch.
eekh shpreh•khuh noor veh•neek ehn•gleesh
Ich spreche kein Englisch.
eekh shpreh•khuh kien ehn•gleesh

I only speak a little English.
I don't speak English.

Write it down, please.	**Bitte schreiben Sie es auf.**
	biht·tuh _shrie_·buhn zee ehs owf
Can you translate this into English for me?	**Können Sie das für mich ins Englische übersetzen?** _ker_·nuhn zee dahs fewr meekh ihns _ehn_·glee·shuh ew·behr·_zeh_·tsuhn
What does… mean?	**Was bedeutet …?** vahs beh·_doyt_·eht …
I understand.	**Ich verstehe.** eekh fehr·_shteh_·uh
I don't understand.	**Ich verstehe nicht.** eekh fehr·_shteh_·uh neekht
Do you understand?	**Verstehen Sie?** fehr·_shteh_·uhn zee

Making Friends

Hello!	**Hallo!** hah·_loh_
Good morning.	**Guten Morgen.** _goo_·tuhn _mohr_·guhn
Good afternoon.	**Guten Tag.** _goo_·tuhn tahk
Good evening.	**Guten Abend.** _goo_·tuhn _ah_·behnt
My name is…	**Mein Name ist …** mien _nahm_·uh ihst …
What's your name?	**Wie heißen Sie?** vee _hie_·sehn zee
I'd like to introduce you to…	**Ich möchte Sie gern … vorstellen.** eekh _merkh_·tuh zee gehrn … fohr·_shteh_·luhn
Pleased to meet you.	**Angenehm.** _ahn_·guh·nehm

| How are you? | **Wie geht es Ihnen?** *vee geht ehs <u>eehn</u>•uhn* |
| Fine, thanks. And you? | **Gut, danke. Und Ihnen?** *goot <u>dahn</u>•kuh oont <u>eehn</u>•uhn* |

> In Germany, it's polite to shake hands, both when you meet and say goodbye. Relatives and close friends may hug or kiss cheeks.

Travel talk

I'm here on business.	**Ich bin geschäftlich hier.** *eekh bihn guh•<u>shehft</u>•leekh heer*
I'm here on vacation	**Ich mache hier Urlaub.** *eekh <u>mahkh</u>•uh heer <u>oor</u>•lowb*
I'm studying here.	**Ich bin zum Studieren hier.** *eekh bihn tsoom <u>shtoo</u>•dee•ruhn heer*
I'm staying for...	**Ich bleibe ...** *eekh <u>blie</u>•buh ...*
I've been here...	**Ich bin seit ... hier.** *eekh been ziet ... heer*
a day	**einem Tag** *<u>ien</u>•uhm tahk*
a week	**einer Woche** *<u>ien</u>•uhr <u>voh</u>•khuh*
a month	**einem Monat** *<u>ien</u>•uhm <u>moh</u>•naht*
Where are you from?	**Woher kommen Sie?** *<u>voh</u>•hehr <u>koh</u>•muhn zee*
I'm from...	**Ich komme aus ...** *eekh <u>koh</u>•muh ows ...*

For Numbers, see page 165.

Personal

Who are you with?	**Mit wem sind Sie hier?** *miht vehm zihnt zee heer*
I'm here alone.	**Ich bin allein hier.** *eekh bihn ah•<u>lien</u> heer*
How old are you?	**Wie alt sind Sie?** *vee ahlt zihnt zee*
I'm...	**Ich bin ...** *eekh bihn ...*

I'm with…	**Ich bin mit … hier.** *eekh been miht … heer*
my husband/wife	**meinem Mann/meiner Frau** <u>*mie*</u>*·nuhm mahn/* <u>*mie*</u>*·nuhr frow*
my boyfriend/	**meinem Freund/meiner Freundin**
my girlfriend	<u>*mie*</u>*·nuhm froynt/*<u>*mie*</u>*·nuhr* <u>*froyn*</u>*·dihn*
my friend	**meinem Freund** <u>*mie*</u>*·nuhm froynt*
my friends	**meinen Freunden** <u>*mie*</u>*·nuhn* <u>*froyn*</u>*·duhn*
my colleague	**meinem Kollegen** <u>*mie*</u>*·nuhm* <u>*koh*</u>*·leh·guhn*
my colleagues	**meinen Kollegen** <u>*mie*</u>*·nuhn* <u>*koh*</u>*·leh·guhn*
When's your birthday?	**Wann haben Sie Geburtstag?** *vahn* <u>*hah*</u>*·buhn zee guh·*<u>*boorts*</u>*·tahk*
Are you married?	**Sind Sie verheiratet?** *zihnt zee fehr·*<u>*hie*</u>*·rah·tuht*
I'm…	**Ich bin …** *eekh bihn …*
single/in a	**ledig/in einer Beziehung** *leh·deek/ihn*
relationship	<u>*ien*</u>*·uhr beh·tsee·oong*
engaged	**verlobt** *fehr·*<u>*lohbt*</u>
married	**verheiratet** *fehr·*<u>*hie*</u>*·rah·tuht*
divorced	**geschieden** *geh·*<u>*shee*</u>*·dehn*
separated	**getrennt lebend** *geh·*<u>*trehnt*</u> *leh·buhnd*
widowed	**verwitwet** *fehr·*<u>*viht*</u>*·veht*
Do you have children/ grandchildren?	**Haben Sie Kinder/Enkelkinder?** <u>*hah*</u>*·buhn zee* <u>*kihn*</u>*·dehr/*<u>*ehn*</u>*·kehl·kihn·dehr*

For Numbers, see page 165.

Work & School

What are you studying?	**Was studieren Sie?** *vahs shtoo·*<u>*dee*</u>*·ruhn zee*
I'm studying German.	**Ich studiere Deutsch.** *eekh shtoo·*<u>*dee*</u>*·ruh doych*
What do you do for a living?	**Was machen Sie beruflich?** *vahs* <u>*mah*</u>*·khuhn zee beh·*<u>*roof*</u>*·leekh*

I . . .	**Ich . . .** *eekh . . .*
work full-time/	**arbeite Vollzeit/Teilzeit** *ahr·bie·tuh*
part-time	*fohl·tsiet/tiel·tsiet*
do freelance work	**bin Freiberufler** *bihn frie·beh·roo·flehr*
am a consultant	**bin Berater** *bihn beh·rah·tehr*
am unemployed	**bin arbeitslos** *bihn ahr·biets·lohs*
work at home	**arbeite zu Hause** *ahr·bie·tuh tsoo how·zuh*
Who do you	**Für wen arbeiten Sie?** *fewr vehn*
work for?	*ahr·bie·tuhn zee*
I work for. . .	**Ich arbeite für . . .** *eekh ahr·bie·tuh fewr . . .*
Here's my business	**Hier ist meine Visitenkarte.** *heer ihst*
card.	*mie·nuh vih·zee·tuhn·kahr·tuh*

For Business Travel, see page 137.

Weather

What's the forecast?	**Wie ist die Wettervorhersage?**
	vee ihst dee veh·tehr·fohr·hehr·zahg·uh
What beautiful/	**Was für ein schönes/schlechtes Wetter!**
terrible weather!	*vahs fewr ien sher·nuhs/shlehkht·uhs veh·tehr*
It's. . .	**Es ist . . .** *ehs ihst . . .*
cool/warm	**kühl/warm** *kewl/vahrm*
cold/hot	**kalt/heiß** *kahlt/hies*
rainy/sunny	**regnerisch/sonnig** *rehg·nuh·reesh/zoh·neek*
There is snow/ice.	**Es gibt Schnee/Eis.** *ehs gihbt shneh/ies*
Do I need a jacket/	**Brauche ich eine Jacke/einen Regenschirm?**
an umbrella?	*brow·khuh eekh ien·uh yah·kuh/*
	ien·uhn reh·guhn·sheerm

For Temperature, see page 171.

ESSENTIAL

Would you like to go out for a drink/dinner?	**Möchten Sie mit mir auf einen Drink/zum Essen gehen?** _merkh_•tuhn zee miht meer owf _ien_•uhn treenk/tsoom _eh_•suhn _geh_•uhn
What are your plans for tonight/tomorrow?	**Was haben Sie heute Abend/morgen vor?** vahs _hah_•buhn zee _hoy_•tuh _ah_•buhnt/_mohr_•guhn fohr
Can I have your number?	**Kann ich Ihre Telefonnummer haben?** kahn eekh _ee_•ruh teh•leh•_fohn_•noo•mehr _hah_•buhn
Can I join you?	**Kann ich mitkommen?** kahn eekh _miht_•koh•muhn
Can I get you a drink?	**Darf ich Ihnen einen Drink ausgeben?** dahrf eekh _eehn_•uhn _ien_•uhn treenk _ows_•geh•buhn
I like/love you.	**Ich mag/liebe dich.** eekh mahk/_lee_•buh deekh

The Dating Game

Would you like to go out… for coffee?	**Möchten Sie mit mir Kaffee trinken gehen?** _mehrkh_•tuhn zee miht meer _ien_•uhn kah•_feh_ _trihnk_•uhn _geh_•uhn
Would you like to go out for a drink?	**Möchten Sie mit mir etwas trinken gehen?** merkht•uhn zee eht•vahs thrihn•khun geh•huhn
Would you like to go out for dinner?	**Möchten Sie mit mir etwas essen gehen?** merkht•uhn zee eht•vahs ehs•suhn geh•huhn
What are your plans for… ?	**Was haben Sie … vor?** vahs _hah_•buhn zee … fohr
today	**heute** _hoy_•tuh
tonight	**heute Abend** _hoy_•tuh _ah_•buhnt
tomorrow	**morgen** _mohr_•guhn
this weekend	**dieses Wochenende** _dee_•zuhs voh•khuhn•_ehn_•duh

Where would you like to go?	**Wohin möchten Sie gern gehen?** _voh_•hihn _merkh_•tuhn zee gehrn _geh_•uhn
I'd like to go…	**Ich möchte gern … gehen.** eekh _merkh_•tuh gehrn … _geh_•uhn
Do you like…?	**Mögen Sie …?** _mer_•guhn zee …
Can I have your number/e-mail?	**Kann ich Ihre Telefonnummer/E-Mail haben?** kahn eekh _ee_•ruh teh•leh•_fohn_•noo•mehr/ _ee_•mehl _hah_•buhn
Are you on Facebook/Twitter?	**Sind Sie bei Facebook/Twitter? (polite form)** zihnt zee by face•book/twit•ter
Can I join you?	**Kann ich mitkommen?** kahn eekh _miht_•koh•muhn
You're very attractive.	**Sie sind sehr attraktiv.** zee zihnt zehr aht•rahk•_teef_
Let's go somewhere quieter.	**Lassen Sie uns an einen ruhigeren Ort gehen.** _lah_•suhn zee oons ahn _ien_•uhn _roo_•ee•geh•ruhn ohrt _geh_•uhn

For Communications, see page 49.

Accepting & Rejecting

| I'd love to. | **Gerne.** _gehr_•nuh |
| Where should we meet? | **Wo wollen wir uns treffen?** voh _voh_•luhn veer oons _treh_•fuhn |

I'll meet you at the bar/your hotel.	**Ich treffe Sie an der Bar/Ihrem Hotel.** *eekh treh·fuh zee ahn dehr bahr/ee·ruhm hoh·tehl*
I'll come by at…	**Ich komme um … vorbei.** *eekh koh·muh oom … fohr·bie*
What is your address?	**Wie ist Ihre Adresse?** *vee ihsht ee·ruh ah·drehs·uh*
I'm busy.	**Ich bin beschäftigt.** *eekh been beh·shehf·teekt*
I'm not interested.	**Ich habe kein Interesse.** *eekh hah·buh kien ihn·teh·reh·suh*
Leave me alone.	**Lassen Sie mich in Ruhe.** *lah·sehn zee meekh ihn roo·uh*
Stop bothering me!	**Hören Sie auf, mich zu belästigen!** *her·ruhn zee owf meekh tsoo buh·lay·steeg·uhn*

For Time, see page 166.

Getting Intimate

Can I hug/kiss you?	**Kann ich dich umarmen/küssen?** *kahn eekh deekh oom·ahr·muhn/kew·zuhn*
Yes.	**Ja.** *yah*
No.	**Nein.** *nien*
Stop!	**Stopp!** *shtohp*
I like/love you.	**Ich mag/liebe dich.** *eekh mahk/lee·buh deekh*

Sexual Preferences

Are you gay?	**Bist du schwul?** *beesht doo shvool*
I'm…	**Ich bin …** *eekh been …*
heterosexual	**heterosexuell** *heh·tuh·roh·sehks·oo·ehl*
homosexual	**homosexuell** *hoh·moh·sehks·oo·ehl*
bisexual	**bisexuell** *bee·sehks·oo·ehl*
Do you like men/women?	**Magst du Männer/Frauen?** *mahgst doo meh·nehr/frow·uhn*

Leisure Time

Sightseeing   105
Shopping   109
Sport & Leisure 125
Going Out   132

Sightseeing

ESSENTIAL

Where's the tourist information office?	**Wo ist das Touristeninformationsbüro?** *voh ihst dahs too·ree·stuhn·een·fohr·mah·syohns·bew·roh*
What are the main sights?	**Was sind die wichtigsten Sehenswürdigkeiten?** *vahs zihnt dee veekh·teeg·stuhn zeh·uhns·vewr·deekh·kie·tuhn*
Do you offer tours in English?	**Haben Sie Führungen in Englisch?** *hah·buhn zee few·roong·uhn een ehn·gleesh*
Can I have a map/ guide?	**Kann ich einen Stadtplan/Reiseführer haben?** *kahn eekh ien·uhn shtaht·plahn/ rie·seh·fewhr·ehr hah·buhn*

Tourist Information

Do you have information on...?	**Haben Sie Informationen über ...?** *hah·buhn zee ihn·fohr·mah·syoh·nuhn ew·buhr ...*
Can you recommend...?	**Können Sie ... empfehlen?** *ker·nuhn zee ... ehm·pfeh·luhn*
a bus tour	**eine Busreise** *ien·uh boos·rie·zuh*
an excursion to...	**einen Ausflug nach ...** *ien·uhn ows·flook nahkh ...*
a sightseeing tour	**eine Stadtrundfahrt** *ien·uh shtaht·roond·fahrt*

On Tour

I'd like to go on the tour to...	**Ich möchte gern an der ... Führung teilnehmen.** *eekh merkht·uh gehrn ahn dehr ... fewhr·oong tiel·nehm·uhn*
When's the next tour?	**Wann ist die nächste Führung?** *vahn ihst dee nehkhst·uh fewhr·oong*

Tourist information offices are located throughout Germany. Look for the 'i' symbol or ask your hotel concierge where the nearest office is located. Tourist information offices can recommend destinations, attractions, local events and festivals, and help you find hotels, tours, transportation and other services. Visit the **Deutsche Zentrale für Tourismus**, **DZT** (German center for tourism), website for more information.

Are there tours in English?	**Gibt es Führungen in Englisch?** *gihpt ehs* *fewhr•oong•uhn ihn ehng•lihsh*
Is there an English guide book/audio guide?	**Gibt es einen englischsprachigen Reiseführer/Audio-Guide?** *gihpt ehs ien•uhn ehng•lihsh•shprahkh•ee•guhn riez•uh•fewhr•ehr/ ow•dee•oh•gied*
What time do we leave/return?	**Wann fahren wir ab/kommen wir wieder?** *vahn fahhr•uhn veer ap/kohm•uhn veer veed•ehr*
We'd like to see…	**Wir möchten gern … sehen.** *veer merkht•uhn gehrn … zeh•uhn*
Can we stop here…?	**Können wir hier anhalten …?** *ker•nuhn veer heer ahn•hahlt•uhn …*
to take photos	**um Fotos zu machen** *oom foht•ohs tsoo mahkh•uhn*
for souvenirs	**um Andenken zu kaufen** *oom ahn•dehnk•uhn tsoo kowf•uhn*
for the toilets	**um auf die Toilette zu gehen** *oom owf dee toy•leht•uh tsoo geh•uhn*
Is it disabled -accessible?	**Ist es behindertengerecht?** *ihst ehs beh•hihn•dehrt•uhn•geh•rehkht*

For Tickets, see page 19.

Seeing the Sights

Where's...?	**Wo ist ...?** *voh ihst ...*
the battleground	**das Schlachtfeld** *dahs shlahkht-fehlt*
the botanical garden	**der botanische Garten** *dehr boh-tahn-eesh-uh gahr-tuhn*
the castle	**das Schloss** *dahs shlohs*
the downtown area	**das Stadtzentrum** *dahs shtadt-tsehnt-room*
the fountain	**der Brunnen** *dehr broon-uhn*
the library	**die Bücherei** *dee bewkh-eh-rie*
the market	**der Markt** *dehr mahrkt*
the museum	**das Museum** *dahs moo-zeh-oom*
the old town	**die Altstadt** *dee ahlt-shtahdt*
the opera house	**das Opernhaus** *dahs oh-pehrn-hows*
the palace	**der Palast** *dehr pah-lahst*
the park	**der Park** *dehr pahrk*
the ruins	**die Ruine** *dee ro-ee-nuh*
the shopping area	**das Einkaufszentrum** *dahs ien-kowfs-tsehn-troom*
the theater	**das Theater** *dahs teh-ah-tehr*
the tower	**der Turm** *dehr toorm*
the town hall	**das Rathaus** *dahs raht-hows*
the town square	**der Rathausplatz** *dehr raht-hows-plats*
Can you show me on the map?	**Können Sie mir das im Stadtplan zeigen?** *ker-nuhn zee meer dahs ihm shtadt-plahn tsie-guhn*
It's...	**Es ist ...** *ehs ihst ...*
amazing	**erstaunlich** *ehr-shtown-leekh*
beautiful	**wunderschön** *voond-ehr-shern*
boring	**langweilig** *lahng-viel-eek*
interesting	**interessant** *ihn-teh-reh-sahnt*
magnificent	**großartig** *groh-sahr-teek*
romantic	**romantisch** *roh-mahnt-eesh*
strange	**seltsam** *zehlt-zahm*

stunning	**umwerfend** <u>oom</u>·vehrf·uhnt
terrible	**schrecklich** <u>shrehk</u>·leekh
ugly	**hässlich** <u>hehs</u>·leekh
I (don't) like it.	**Es gefällt mir (nicht).** ehs guh·<u>fehlt</u> meer (neekht)

For Asking Directions, see page 34.

Religious Sites

Where's ...?	**Wo ist ...?** voh ihst ...
the cathedral	**die Kathedrale** dee kah·teh·<u>drahl</u>·uh
the Catholic/	**die katholische/evangelische Kirche**
Protestant church	dee kah·<u>toh</u>·leesh·uh/eh·vahn·<u>gehl</u>·eesh·uh <u>keer</u>·khuh
the mosque	**die Moschee** dee moh·<u>sheh</u>
the shrine	**der Schrein** dehr shrien
the synagogue	**die Synagoge** dee zewn·uh·<u>goh</u>·guh
the temple	**der Tempel** dehr <u>tehm</u>·pehl
What time is mass/	**Wann ist die Messe/der Gottesdienst?**
the service?	vahn ihst dee <u>mehs</u>·suh/dehr <u>goht</u>·ehs·deenst

Shopping

Shopping
109

ESSENTIAL

Where's the market/mall [shopping centre]?	**Wo ist der Markt/das Einkaufszentrum?** *voh ihst dehr mahrkt/dahs ien•kowfs•tsehn•troom*
I'm just looking.	**Ich schaue mich nur um.** *eekh show•uh meekh noor oom*
Can you help me?	**Können Sie mir helfen?** *kern•uhn zee meer hehlf•uhn*
I'm being helped.	**Ich werde schon bedient.** *eekh vehrd•uh shohn beh•deent*
How much?	**Wie viel kostet das?** *vee feel kohs•tuht dahs*
That one, please.	**Dieses bitte.** *dee•zuhs biht•tuh*
That's all.	**Das ist alles.** *dahs ihst ahl•uhs*
Where can I pay?	**Wo kann ich bezahlen?** *voh kahn eekh beh•tsahl•uhn*
I'll pay in cash/by credit card.	**Ich zahle bar/mit Kreditkarte.** *eekh tsahl•uh bahr/miht kreh•deet•kahr•tuh*
A receipt, please.	**Eine Quittung, bitte.** *ien•uh kvih•toong biht•tuh*

At the Shops

Where's...?	**Wo ist ...?** *voh ihst ...*
the antiques store	**das Antiquitätengeschäft** *dahs ahn•tee•kwee•tay•tuhn•guh•shehft*
the bakery	**die Bäckerei** *dee beh•keh•rie*
the bank	**die Bank** *dee bahnk*
the bookstore	**der Buchladen** *dehr bookh•lahd•uhn*

the clothing store	**das Bekleidungsgeschäft**
	dahs buh·klied·oongs·guh·shehft
the delicatessen	**das Feinkostgeschäft** *dahs fien·kohst·guh·shehft*
the department store	**das Kaufhaus** *dahs kowf·hows*
the gift shop	**der Geschenkwarenladen**
	dehr guh·shehnk·vah·ruhn·lah·duhn
the health food store	**das Reformhaus** *dahs reh·fohrm·hows*
the jeweler	**das Schmuckgeschäft** *dahs shmook·guh·shehft*
the liquor store [off-licence]	**das Spirituosengeschäft**
	dahs shpee·ree·twoh·zuhn·guh·shehft
the market	**der Markt** *dehr mahrkt*
the music store	**das Musikgeschäft** *dahs moo·zeek·guh·shehft*
the pastry shop	**die Konditorei** *dee kohn·dee·toh·rie*
the pharmacy [chemist]	**die Apotheke** *dee ah·poh·tehk·uh*
the produce [grocery] store	**das Lebensmittelgeschäft**
	dahs lehb·uhns·miht·uhl·guh·shehft
the shoe store	**das Schuhgeschäft** *dahs shooh·guh·shehft*
the shopping mall [shopping centre]	**das Einkaufszentrum**
	dahs ien·kowfs·tsehn·troom
the souvenir store	**der Andenkenladen** *dehr ahn·dehnk·uhn·lah·duhn*
the supermarket	**der Supermarkt** *dehr zoo·pehr·mahrkt*
the tobacconist	**der Tabakladen** *dehr tah·bahk·lahd·uhn*
the toy store	**das Spielzeuggeschäft** *dahs shpeel·tsoyg·geh·shehft*

Ask an Assistant

When do you open/close?	**Wann öffnen/schließen Sie?** *vahn erf·nuhn/ shlees·uhn zee*
Where's ...?	**Wo ist ...?** *voh ihst ...*

the cashier	**die Kasse** *dee kah•suh*
the escalator	**die Rolltreppe** *dee rohl•trehp•uh*
the elevator [lift]	**der Fahrstuhl** *dehr fahr•shtool*
the fitting room	**die Umkleidekabine** *dee oom•klied•uh•kah•bee•nuh*
the store directory	**die Liste mit den Geschäften?**
	dee lihs•tuh miht dehn guh•sheft•tuhn
Can you help me?	**Können Sie mir helfen?** *kern•uhn zee meer hehl•fuhn*
I'm just looking.	**Ich schaue mich nur um.** *eekh show•uh*
	meekh noor oom
I'm already being	**Ich werde schon bedient.** *eekh vehrd•uh*
helped.	*shohn buh•deent*
Do you have…?	**Haben Sie …?** *hah•buhn zee …*

YOU MAY SEE...

GEÖFFNET/GESCHLOSSEN	open/closed
ÜBER MITTAG GESCHLOSSEN	closed for lunch
EINGANG	entrance
UMKLEIDEKABINE	fitting room
KASSE	cashier
NUR BARZAHLUNG MÖGLICH	cash only
KREDITKARTENZAHLUNG MÖGLICH	credit cards accepted
ÖFFNUNGSZEITEN	business hours
AUSGANG	exit

Can you show me...?	**Können Sie mir ... zeigen?**	_kern_•nuhn zee meer ... _tsieg_•uhn
Can you ship/wrap it?	**Können Sie das versenden/einpacken?**	_kern_•uhn zee dahs fehr•_zehn_•duhn/_ien_•pahk•uhn
How much?	**Wie viel kostet es?**	vee feel _kohs_•tuht ehs
That's all.	**Das ist alles.**	dahs ihst _ahl_•uhs

For Clothing, see page 117.

For Meals & Cooking, see page 67.

For Souvenirs, see page 123.

Personal Preferences

I'd like something...	**Ich möchte etwas ...**	eekh _merkht_•uh _eht_•vahs ...
cheap/expensive	**Billiges/Teueres**	_bihl_•ee•guhs/_toy_•ehr•uhs
larger/smaller	**Größeres/Kleineres**	_grers_•eh•ruhs/_klien_•eh•ruhs
nicer	**Schöneres**	_shern_•uh•ruhs
from this region	**aus dieser Region**	ows _deez_•ehr rehg•_yohn_
Around...euros.	**Ungefähr ... Euro.**	_oon_•guh•fehr ... _oy_•roh
Can you show me...?	**Können Sie mir ... zeigen?**	_kern_•uhn zee meer ... _tsieg_•uhn

Is it real?	**Ist das echt?** *ihst dahs ehkht*
That's not quite what I want.	**Das ist nicht ganz das, was ich möchte.** *dahs ihst neekht gahnts dahs vahs eekh merkht•uh*
No, I don't like it.	**Das gefällt mir nicht.** *dahs guh•fehlt meer neekht*
It's too expensive.	**Es ist zu teuer.** *ehs ihst tsoo toy•ehr*
I have to think about it.	**Das muss ich mir überlegen.** *dahs moos eekh meer ewb•ehr•leh•guhn*
I'll take it.	**Ich nehme es.** *eekh nehm•uh ehs*

Paying & Bargaining

How much?	**Wie viel kostet es?** *vee feel kohs•tuht ehs*
I'll pay...	**Ich zahle ...** *eekh tsah•luh ...*
in cash	**bar** *bahr*
by credit card	**mit Kreditkarte** *miht kreh•deet•kahr•tuh*
by traveler's cheque	**mit Reiseschecks** *miht riez•uh•shehks*
A receipt, please.	**Die Quittung, bitte.** *dee kviht•oong biht•tuh*
That's too much.	**Das ist zu viel.** *dahs ihst tsoo veel*
I'll give you...	**Ich gebe Ihnen ...** *eekh gehb•uh eehn•uhn ...*
I have only... euros.	**Ich habe nur ... Euro.** *eekh hah•buh noor ... oy•roh*

In Germany, cash is the preferred form of payment. Credit cards are accepted in most larger stores, gas stations, hotels and restaurants. Credit cards may not be accepted by smaller businesses, so be sure to ask before making a purchase. Traveler's checks are not very popular in Germany. If taken, they should be exchanged for cash at a currency exchange office or bank, though a fee will be charged for the exchange. Some banks do not accept traveler's checks.

YOU MAY HEAR...

Wie möchten Sie zahlen? *vee merkht•uhn zee tsahl•uhn*

How are you paying?

Ihre Kreditkarte wurde abgelehnt. *eehr•uh kreh•deet•kahr•tuh voor•duh ahp•guh•lehnt*

Your credit card has been declined.

Ihren Ausweis, bitte. *eehr•uhn ows•vies biht•tuh*

ID, please.

Wir nehmen keine Kreditkarten. *veer neh•muhn kie•nuh kreh•deet•kahr•tuhn*

We don't accept credit cards.

Bitte nur Bargeld. *biht•tuh noor bahr•gehlt*

Cash only, please.

Haben Sie Wechselgeld/kleine Scheine? *hah•buhn zee vehkh•zuhl•gehlt/klien•uh shien•uh*

Do you have change/ small bills [notes]?

Is that your best price?	**Ist das Ihr bester Preis?** *ihst dahs eehr behst•ehr pries*
Can you give me a discount?	**Können Sie mir einen Rabatt geben?** *kern•uhn zee meer ien•uhn rah•baht geh•buhn*

For Numbers, see page 165.

Making a Complaint

I'd like...	**Ich möchte ...** *eekh merkht•uh ...*
to exchange this	**das umtauschen** *dahs oom•tow•shuhn*
a refund	**gern mein Geld zurück** *gehrn mien gehld tsoo•rewk*
to see the manager	**mit dem Manager sprechen** *miht dehm mahn•ah•jehr shprehkh•uhn*

Services

Can you recommend…?	**Können Sie … empfehlen?** _kern_·uhn zee … ehm·_pfeh_·luhn
a barber	**einen Herrenfriseur** _ien_·uhn _hehr_·uhn·frih·zer
a dry cleaner	**eine Reinigung** _ien_·uh _rien_·ee·goong
a hairstylist	**einen Friseur** _ien_·uhn frih·_zer_
a laundromat [launderette]	**einen Waschsalon** _ien_·uhn _vahsh_·zah·lohn
a nail salon	**ein Nagelstudio** ien _nah_·gehl·shtood·yoh
a spa	**ein Wellness-Center** ien _vehl_·nuhs·_sehn_·tehr
a travel agency	**ein Reisebüro** ien _rie_·zuh·bew·roh
Can you…this?	**Können Sie das …?** _kern_·uhn zee dahs …
alter	**ändern** _ehn_·dehrn
clean	**reinigen** _rien_·ee·guhn
fix	**reparieren** reh·pah·_reer_·uhn
press	**bügeln** _bewg_·uhln
When will it be ready?	**Wann wird es fertig sein?** vahn veerd ehs _fehr_·teekh zien

Hair & Beauty

I'd like…	**Ich möchte …** eekh _merkht_·uh …
an appointment for today/tomorrow	**einen Termin für heute/morgen** _ien_·uhn tehr·_meen_ fewr _hoy_·tuh/_mohr_·guhn
some color/ highlights	**die Haare/Strähnchen gefärbt bekommen** dee _hah_·ruh/_shtrehnkh_·uhn guh·_ferbt_ buh·_kohm_·uhn
my hair styled/ blow-dried	**mein Haar stylen/fönen lassen** mien hahr _shtew_·luhn/_fern_·uhn _lahs_·uhn
a haircut	**einen Haarschnitt** _ien_·uhn _hahr_·shniht
an eyebrow/bikini wax	**eine Haarentfernung an den Augenbrauen /der Bikinizone** _ien_·uh _hahr_·ehnt·fehr·noong ahn dehn _ow_·guhn·brow·uhn/dehr bee·_kee_·nee·tsoh·nuh

a facial	**eine Gesichtsbehandlung**
	ien•uh guh•zeekhts•beh•hahnd•loong
a manicure/ pedicure	**eine Maniküre/Pediküre** _ien•uh_
	mahn•eh•kewruh/pede•eh•kewruh
a (sports) massage	**eine (Sport-)Massage** _ien•uh (shport-) mah•sahdj•uh_
a trim	**die Haare nachschneiden lassen**
	dee hahr•uh nahkh•shnayd•uhn lahs•uhn
Not too short.	**Nicht zu kurz.** _neekht tsoo koorts_
Shorter here.	**Hier kürzer.** _heer kewrts•ehr_
Do you offer...?	**Machen Sie ...?** _mahk•uhn zee ..._
acupuncture	**Akupunktur** _ah•koo•poonk•toor_
aromatherapy	**Aromatherapie** _ah•roh•mah•teh•rah•pee_
oxygen treatment	**Sauerstoffbehandlung**
	zow•ehr•shtohf•beh•hahnd•loong
Do you have a sauna?	**Haben Sie eine Sauna?** _hah•buhn zee ien•uh zown•ah_

Health resorts, day spas and hotel spas are popular destinations, and there are hundreds throughout Germany. Most spa towns have the word **Bad** in their names, for example: Bad Reichenhall, Europe's largest saline source, in Bavaria; Baden-Baden, considered the best and most fashionable; Wiesbaden, one of Germany's oldest cities and considered second best only to Baden-Baden; Bad Homburg, at the foot of Taunus Hills, once the summer retreat of Prussian kings; and Bad Nauheim, famous because both William Randolph Hearst and Elvis Presley were once guests experiencing the healing powers of the carbonic acid springs.

Tipping varies by spa; ask about the tipping policy when booking or upon arrival.

Antiques

How old is it?	**Wie alt ist es?** *vee ahlt ihst ehs*
Do you have anything from the…period?	**Haben Sie etwas aus der … Zeit?** *hah•buhn zee eht•vahs ows dehr … tsiet*
Do I have to fill out any forms?	**Muss ich irgendwelche Formulare ausfüllen?** *moos eekh eer•guhnd•vehlkh•uh fohr•moo•lahr•uh ows•fewl•uhn*
Is there a certificate of authenticity?	**Gibt es ein Echtheitszeugnis?** *gihpt ehs ien ehkht•hiets•tsoyg•nuhs*
Can you ship/wrap it?	**Können Sie es liefern/einpacken?** *ker•nuhn zee ehs lee•fuhrn/ien•pahk•kuhn*

Clothing

I'd like…	**Ich möchte …** *eekh merkht•uh …*
Can I try this on?	**Kann ich das anprobieren?** *kahn eekh dahs ahn•proh•bee•ruhn*
It doesn't fit.	**Es passt nicht.** *ehs pahst neekht*
It's too…	**Es ist zu …** *ehs ihst tsoo …*
big/small	**groß/klein** *grohs/klien*
short/long	**kurz/lang** *koorts/lahng*
tight/loose	**eng/weit** *ehng/viet*

Do you have this in size...?	**Haben Sie das in der Größe ... ?** _hah•buhn zee dahs ihn dehr grers•uh ..._
Do you have this in a bigger/smaller size?	**Haben Sie das in einer größeren/kleineren Größe?** _hah•buhn zee dahs ihn ien•ehr grers•ehr•uhn/klien•uh•ruhn grers•uh_

For Numbers, see page 165.

Colors

I'd like something...	**Ich möchte etwas ...** _eekh merkht•uh eht•vahs ..._
beige	**Beiges** _behdj•uhs_
black	**Schwarzes** _shvahrtz•uhs_
blue	**Blaues** _blow•uhs_
brown	**Braunes** _brown•uhs_
green	**Grünes** _grewn•uhs_
gray	**Graues** _grow•uhs_
orange	**Oranges** _oh•rahnj•uhs_
pink	**Pinkes** _peenk•uhs_
purple	**Violettes** _vee•oh•leht•uhs_
red	**Rotes** _roht•uhs_
white	**Weißes** _vies•uhs_
yellow	**Gelbes** _gehlb•uhs_

Clothes & Accessories

a backpack	**der Rucksack** *dehr rook·zahk*
a belt	**der Gürtel** *dehr gewrt·uhl*
a bikini	**der Bikini** *dehr bih·kee·nee*
a blouse	**die Bluse** *dee bloo·zuh*
a bra	**der BH** *dehr beh·hah*
briefs [underpants]	**der Schlüpfer** *dehr shlewp·fehr*
panties	**die Unterhosen** *dee oont·ehr·hoh·suhn*
a coat	**der Mantel** *dehr mahnt·ehl*
a dress	**das Kleid** *dahs klied*
a hat	**der Hut** *dehr hoot*
a jacket	**die Jacke** *dee yah·kuh*

YOU MAY HEAR...

Das steht Ihnen gut.
dahs shteht eehn·uhn goot

That looks great on you.

Passt es? *pahst ehs*

How does it fit?

Wir führen Ihre Größe nicht.
veer fewhr·uhn eehr·uh grers·uh neekht

We don't have your
size.

jeans	**die Jeans** *dee djeens*
pajamas	**der Schlafanzug** *dehr shlahf•ahn•tsoog*
pants [trousers]	**die Hose** *dee hohz•uh*
pantyhose [tights]	**die Strumpfhose** *dee shtroompf•hoh•zuh*
a purse [handbag]	**die Handtasche** *dee hahnd•tahsh•uh*
a raincoat	**der Regenmantel** *dehr rehg•uhn•mahn•tuhl*
a scarf	**der Schal** *dehr shahl*
a shirt	**das Hemd** *dahs hehmt*
shorts	**die kurze Hose** *dee koortz•uh hohz•uh*
a skirt	**der Rock** *dehr rohk*
socks	**die Socken** *dee zohk•uhn*
a suit	**der Anzug** *dehr ahn•tsoog*
sunglasses	**die Sonnenbrille** *dee zohn•uhn•brihl•uh*
a sweater	**der Pullover** *dehr pool•oh•fehr*
a sweatshirt	**das Sweatshirt** *dahs sveht•shehrt*
a swimsuit	**der Badeanzug** *dehr bah•deh•ahn•tsoog*
a T-shirt	**das T-Shirt** *dahs tee•shert*
a tie	**die Krawatte** *dee krah•vah•tuh*
underwear	**die Unterwäsche** *dee oon•tehr•vehsh•uh*

Fabric

I'd like…	**Ich möchte …** *eekh merkht•uh …*
cotton	**Baumwolle** *bowm•vohl•uh*
denim	**Denim** *dehn•ihm*
lace	**Spitze** *shpihts•uh*
leather	**Leder** *lehd•ehr*
linen	**Leinen** *lien•uhn*
silk	**Seide** *zied•uh*
wool	**Wolle** *vohl•uh*
Is it machine washable?	**Ist es waschmaschinenfest?** *ihst ehs vahsh•mah•sheen•uhn•fehst*

Shoes

I'd like...	**Ich möchte ...** *eekh merkht·uh ...*
high-heels/flats	**Schuhe mit Absatz/ohne Absatz** *shoo·uh miht ahp·zahts/ohn·uh ahb·zahts*
boots	**Stiefel** *shtee·fuhl*
loafers	**Slipper** *slihp·ehr*
sandals	**Sandalen** *zahn·dahl·uhn*
shoes	**Schuhe** *shoo·uh*
slippers	**Badelatschen** *bah·duh·lahtsh·uhn*
sneakers	**Turnschuhe** *toorn·shoo·huh*
In size...	**In der Größe ...** *ihn dehr grers·uh ...*

For Numbers, see page 165.

Sizes

small (S)	**klein** *klein*
medium (M)	**mittel** *miht·tuhl*
large (L)	**gross** *grohs*
extra large (XL)	**extra gross** *ehks·trah grohs*
petite	**die Kurzgröße** *dee koorts·grer·suh*
plus size	**die Übergröße** *dee ew·buhr·grer·suh*

Newsagent & Tobacconist

Do you sell English-language newspapers?	**Haben Sie englischsprachige Zeitungen?** *hah·buhn zee ehng·leesh·shprah·khee·guh tsie·toong·uhn*
I'd like...	**Ich möchte ...** *eekh merkht·uh ...*
candy [sweets]	**Süßigkeiten** *zews·eekh·kiet·uhn*
chewing gum	**Kaugummi** *kow·goo·mee*
a chocolate bar	**einen Schokoladenriegel** *ien·uhn shoh·koh·lahd·uhn·ree·guhl*
a cigar	**eine Zigarre** *ien·uh tsee·gahr·uh*

a pack/carton of cigarettes	**eine Schachtel/Stange Zigaretten** _ien_·uh _shahkht_·uhl/_shtahng_·uh tsee·gahr·_eht_·uhn
a lighter	**ein Feuerzeug** ien _foy_·ehr·tsoyg
a magazine	**eine Zeitschrift** _ien_·uh _tsiet_·shrihft
matches	**Streichhölzer** _shtriekh_·herlts·uhr
a newspaper	**eine Zeitung** _ien_·uh _tsie_·toong
a pen	**einen Stift** _ien_·uhn shtihft
a postcard	**eine Postkarte** _ien_·uh _pohst_·kahr·tuh
a road/town map of...	**eine Straßenkarte/einen Stadtplan vonen ...** _ien_·uh _shtrahsuhn_·kahrt·uh/_ien_·uhn _shtaht_·plahn fohn
stamps	**Briefmarken** _breef_·mahrk·uhn

Photography

I'd like a/an... camera.	**Ich möchte eine ... Kamera.** eekh _merkht_·uh _ien_·uh ... _kah_·meh·ruh
automatic	**automatische** ow·toh·_maht_·ihsh·uh
digital	**digitale** _dihd_·juh·tuhl
disposable	**Wegwerf-** _vehk_·vehrf-
I'd like...	**Ich möchte ...** eekh _merkht_·uh ...
a battery	**eine Batterie** _ien_·uh bah·tuh·_ree_
digital prints	**digitale Ausdrucke** _dihd_·juh·tuhl _ows_·drook·uh
a memory card	**eine Speicherkarte** _ien_·uh _shpie_·khuhr·kahrt·uh
Can I print digital photos here?	**Kann ich hier Digitalfotos ausdrucken lassen?** kahn eekh heer dihd·jih·_tahl_·foh·tohs _ows_·droo·kuhn _lahs_·uhn

In addition to small, medium and large, many clothing articles are labeled by continental size. As that size varies by manufacturer, be sure to try on any article before buying.

Souvenirs

Can I see this/that?	**Kann ich das sehen?** *kahn eekh dahs <u>zeh</u>•uhn*
It's in the window/ display case.	**Es ist im Schaufenster/in der Vitrine.** *ehs ihst ihm <u>show</u>•fehn•stehr/ihn dehr vih•<u>tree</u>•nuh*
I'd like...	**Ich möchte ...** *eekh <u>merkht</u>•uh ...*
a battery	**eine Batterie** *<u>ien</u>•uh bah•tuh•<u>ree</u>*
a bracelet	**ein Armband** *ien <u>ahrm</u>•bahnt*
a brooch	**eine Brosche** *<u>ien</u>•uh <u>brohsh</u>•uh*
a clock	**eine Uhr** *<u>ien</u>•uh oohr*
earrings	**Ohrringe** *<u>oh</u>•reeng•uh*
a necklace	**eine Kette** *<u>ien</u>•uh <u>keht</u>•uh*
a ring	**einen Ring** *<u>ien</u>•uhn reeng*
a watch	**eine Uhr** *<u>ien</u>•uh oohr*
I'd like...	**Ich möchte ...** *eekh <u>merkht</u>•uh ...*
a beer stein	**einen Bierkrug** *<u>ien</u>•uh beer•kroog*
a bottle of wine	**eine Flasche Wein** *<u>ien</u>•uh flahsh•uh vien*
a box of chocolates	**eine Schachtel Pralinen** *<u>ien</u>•uh shahkht•uhl prah•lee•nuhn*
a doll	**eine Puppe** *<u>ien</u>•uh poo•puh*
a key ring	**ein Schlüsselring** *<u>ien</u> shlews•uhl•reeng*
a postcard	**eine Postkarte** *<u>ien</u>•uh post•kahr•tuh*

pottery	**Töpferwaren** _terp·fuhr·vah·ruhn_
a T-shirt	**ein T-Shirt** _ien tee·shehrt_
a toy	**ein Spielzeug** _ien shpeel·tsoyg_
copper	**Kupfer** _koop·fehr_
crystal	**Kristall** _krihs·tahl_
diamonds	**Diamanten** _dee·ah·mahn·tuhn_
white/yellow gold	**Weißgold/Gelbgold** _vies·gohlt/gehlb·gohlt_
pearls	**Perlen** _pehr·luhn_
pewter	**Zinn** _tsihn_
platinum	**Platin** _plah·teen_
sterling silver	**Sterlingsilber** _shtehr·leeng·zihl·behr_
Is this real?	**Ist das echt?** _ihst dahs ehkht_
Can you engrave it?	**Können Sie etwas eingravieren?**
	ker·nuhn zee eht·vahs ien·grah·vee·ruhn

One of Germany's most famous products is the Black Forest cuckoo clock. Though very expensive, these clocks will last for generations if properly cared for. Another popular and less expensive souvenir is a traditional German beer stein. Collector beer steins are made from clay, glass or pewter and can be brightly painted, with or without a lid and engraved. Germany is also known for its toys: wooden figurines, porcelain dolls and model trains. Other souvenirs include: **lederhosen** (traditional German pants), lace and porcelain.

ESSENTIAL

When's the game?	**Wann findet das Spiel statt?**
	vahn fihnd•uht dahs shpeel shtaht
Where's…?	**Wo ist … ?** *voh ihst …*
the beach	**der Strand** *dehr shtrahnd*
the park	**der Park** *dehr pahrk*
the pool	**der Pool** *dehr pool*
Is it safe to swim here?	**Kann man hier schwimmen?** *kahn mahn heer shvihm•uhn*
Can I hire golf clubs?	**Kann ich Golfschläger ausleihen?** *kahn eekh gohlf•shlelig•ehr ows•lie•uhn*
How much per hour?	**Wie viel kostet es pro Stunde?** *vee feel kohs•tuht ehs proh shtoond•uh*
How far is it to…?	**Wie weit ist es bis zum *m* /zur *f* …?** *vee viet ihst ehs bihs tsoom /tsoor …*
Show me on the map, please.	**Zeigen Sie es mir bitte auf dem Stadtplan.** *tsieg•uhn zee ehs meer biht•tuh owf dehm shtaht•plahn*

Watching Sport

When's…?	**Wann findet … statt?** *vahn fihnd•uht … shtaht*
the baseball game	**das Baseballspiel** *dahs behs•bahl•shpeel*
the basketball game	**das Basketballspiel** *dahs bahs•kuht•bahl•shpeel*
the boxing match	**der Boxkampf** *dehr bohx•kahmpf*
the cricket match	**das Cricket-Turnier** *dahs krih•kuht•toor•neer*
the cycling race	**das Radrennen** *dahs rahd•rehn•uhn*

the golf tournament	**das Golfturnier** *dahs golf•toor•neer*
the soccer [football] game	**das Fußballspiel** *dahs foos•bahl•shpeel*
the tennis match	**das Tennismatch** *dahs tehn•ihs•mahch*
the volleyball game	**das Volleyballspiel** *dahs voh•lee•bahl•shpeel*
Who's playing?	**Wer spielt?** *vehr shpeelt*
Where's the racetrack/stadium?	**Wo ist die Rennbahn/das Stadion?** *voh ihst dee rehn•bahn/dahs shtah•dyohn*
Where can I place a bet?	**Wo kann ich eine Wette abschließen?** *voh kahn eekh ien•uh veh•tuh ahp•shlees•uhn*

For Tickets, see page 19.

Playing Sport

Where is/are…?	**Wo ist/sind …?** *voh ihst/zihnt …*
the golf course	**der Golfplatz** *dehr golf•plahts*
the gym	**die Sporthalle** *dee shpohrt•hah•luh*
the park	**der Park** *dehr pahrk*
the tennis courts	**die Tennisplätze** *dee tehn•ihs•pleht•suh*
How much per…	**Wie viel kostet es pro …** *vee feel kohs•tuht ehs proh …*
day	**Tag** *tak*
hour	**Stunde** *shtoond•uh*
game	**Spiel** *shpeel*
round	**Runde** *roond•uh*
Can I rent [hire]…?	**Kann ich … ausleihen?** *kahn eekh … ows•lie•huhn*
golf clubs	**Golfschläger** *golf•shlehg•ehr*
equipment	**eine Ausrüstung** *ien•uh ows•rews•toong*
a racket	**einen Schläger** *ien•uhn shlehg•ehr*

Germany's most popular sport is **Fußball** (soccer); in fact, Germany has won the World Cup three times. Tennis is another popular sport; the German Tennis Federation boasts membership of more than one million. Other popular sports include biking, hiking, handball, basketball, volleyball, ice hockey, golf and horseback riding. Casinos are found throughout Germany. The spa towns, in particular, are home to well-known casinos.

At the Beach/Pool

Where's the beach/pool?	**Wo ist der Strand/Pool?** *voh ihst dehr shtrahnt/pool*
Is there a...?	**Gibt es einen ...?** *gihpt ehs <u>ien</u>•uhn ...*
kiddie pool	**Pool für Kinder** *pool fewr <u>kihnd</u>•ehr*
indoor/outdoor pool	**Hallenbad/Freibad** *<u>hahl</u>•ehn•baht/<u>frie</u>•baht*
lifeguard	**Rettungsschwimmer** *<u>reht</u>•oongs•shvihm•ehr*

Germany's main beach areas are located along the North Sea and Baltic Sea coasts. There are numerous types of beaches in Germany, including family, adults-only and nude beaches. A few of the more popular areas include Sylt, known for its nude beaches; Büsum, an intimate small town with calm North Sea waters; Helgoland, a Frisian island in the North Sea; Heiligendamm, Germany's oldest seaside resort; Heringsdorf, on the island of Usedom; and Kühlungsborn and Warnemünde, located on the Baltic Sea.

Is it safe to swim/dive?	**Ist es sicher zu schwimmen/tauchen?** *ihst ehs <u>sihk</u>•hehr tsoo shvihm•uhn/<u>towkh</u>•uhn*
Is it safe for children?	**Ist es kindgerecht?** *ihst ehs <u>kihnt</u>•guh•rehkht*
I'd like to rent hire...	**Ich möchte gern ... ausleihen.** *eekh <u>merkht</u>•uh gehrn ... <u>ows</u>•lie•uhn*
a deck chair	**einen Liegestuhl** *<u>ien</u>•uhn <u>leeg</u>•uh•shtoohl*
diving equipment	**eine Tauchausrüstung** *<u>ien</u>•uh <u>towkh</u>•ows•rew•stoong*
a jet ski	**einen Jet Ski** *<u>ien</u>•uhn djeht skee*
a motorboat	**ein Motorboot** *ien <u>moht</u>•ohr•boht*
a rowboat	**ein Ruderboot** *ien <u>rood</u>•ehr•boht*
snorkeling equipment	**eine Schnorchelausrüstung** *<u>ien</u>•uh <u>shnohr</u>•khehl•ows•rew•stoong*
a surfboard	**ein Surfboard** *ien <u>soorf</u>•bohrd*
a towel	**ein Handtuch** *ien <u>hahnd</u>•tookh*
an umbrella	**einen Schirm** *<u>ien</u>•uhn sheerm*
water skis	**Wasserski** *<u>vahs</u>•ehr•shee*
a windsurfer	**ein Surfbrett** *ien serf•breht*
For...hours.	**Für ... Stunden.** *fewr ... <u>shtoond</u>•uhn*

Winter Sports

A lift pass for a day/ five days, please.	**Einen Liftpass für einen Tag/fünf Tage, bitte.** _ien•uhn lihft•pahs fewr ien•uhn tahk/fewnf tahg•uh biht•tuh_
I'd like to hire...	**Ich möchte gerne ... ausleihen.** _eekh merkht•uh gehr•nuh ... ows•lie•uhn_
boots	**Stiefel** _shteef•uhl_
a helmet	**einen Helm** _ien•uhn hehlm_
poles	**Stöcke** _shterk•uh_
skis	**Skier** _skee•ehr_
a snowboard	**ein Snowboard** _ien snohw•bohrd_
snowshoes	**Schneeschuhe** _shneh•shoo•uh_
These are too big/small.	**Diese sind zu groß/klein.** _dee•zuh zihnt tsoo grohs/klien_

Winter offers plenty of opportunities for outdoor activity in Germany. Alpine skiing, snowboarding, cross-country skiing, ice skating, tobogganing and hiking are just some of the options available to winter travelers.

Are there lessons?	**Kann man Stunden nehmen?**
	kahn mahn <u>shtoond</u>•uhn <u>neh</u>•muhn
I'm a beginner.	**Ich bin Anfänger.** *eekh bihn ahn•<u>fehng</u>•ehr*
I'm experienced.	**Ich bin erfahren.** *eekh been ehr•<u>fahr</u>•uhn*
A trail [piste] map, please.	**Bitte einen Pistenplan.** <u>biht</u>•tuh <u>ien</u>•uhn <u>pees</u>•tuhn•plahn*

YOU MAY SEE...

SCHLEPPLIFT	drag lift
SEILBAHN	cable car
SESSELLIFT	chair lift
ANFÄNGER	novice
FORTGESCHRITTENE	intermediate
KÖNNER	expert
PISTE GESCHLOSSEN	trail [piste] closed

Out in the Country

A map of..., please.	**Eine Karte ..., bitte.** _ien_•uh _kahrt_•uh ... _biht_•tuh
this region	**dieser Region** _deez_•uhr rehg•_yohn_
the walking routes	**mit Wanderrouten** miht _vahnd_•ehr•root•uhn
the bike routes	**mit Radrouten** miht _rahd_•root•uhn
the trails	**mit Wanderwegen** miht _vahnd_•ehr•veh•guhn
Is it...?	**Ist es ...?** ihst ehs ...
easy	**leicht** liekht
difficult	**schwierig** _shveer_•eeg
far	**weit** viet
steep	**steil** shtiel
How far is it to...?	**Wie weit ist es bis ...?** vee viet ihst ehs bihs ...
Show me on the map, please.	**Zeigen Sie es mir bitte auf der Karte.** _tsieg_•uhn zee ehs meer _biht_•tuh owf dehr _kahrt_•uh
I'm lost.	**Ich habe mich verlaufen.** eekh _hahb_•uh meekh fehr•_lowf_•uhn
Where's...?	**Wo ist ...?** voh ihst ...
the bridge	**die Brücke** dee _brew_•kuh
the cave	**die Höhle** dee _her_•luh
the canyon	**der Canyon** dehr _kahn_•yohn
the cliff	**die Klippe** dee _klih_•puh
the desert	**die Wüste?** dee vews•tuh
the farm	**der Bauernhof** dehr _bow_•ehrn•hohf
the field	**das Feld** dahs fehld
the forest	**der Wald** dehr vahld
the hill	**der Hügel** dehr _hew_•gehl
the lake	**der See** dehr zeh
the mountain	**der Berg** dehr behrg
the nature preserve	**das Naturschutzgebiet** dahs _nah_•toor•shoots•guh•beet
the viewpoint	**der Aussichtspunkt** dehr _ows_•seekhts•poonkt

the park	**der Park** *dehr pahrk*
the path	**der Pfad** *dehr pfahd*
the peak	**der Gipfel** *dehr gihp·fuhl*
the picnic area	**der Picknickplatz** *dehr pihk·nihk·plahts*
the pond	**der Teich** *dehr tiekh*
the ravine	**die Schlucht** *dee shlookht*
the river	**der Fluss** *dehr floos*
the sea	**das Meer** *dahs mehr*
the (hot) spring	**die (heiße) Quelle** *dee (hie·suh) kveh·luh*
the stream	**der Strom** *dehr shtrom*
the valley	**das Tal** *dahs tahl*
the village	**das Dorf** *dahs dohrf*
the vineyard	**das Weingut** *dahs vien·goot*
the waterfall	**der Wasserfall** *dehr vahs·ehr·fahl*

Going Out

ESSENTIAL

What's there to do at night?	**Was kann man dort abends unternehmen?** *vahs kahn mahn dohrt ahb·uhnds oon·tehr·nehm·uhn*
Do you have a program of events?	**Haben Sie ein Veranstaltungsprogramm?** *hah·buhn zee ien fehr·ahn·shtahlt·oongs·prohg·rahm*
What's playing tonight?	**Was wird heute Abend aufgeführt?** *vahs vihrd hoyt·uh ahb·uhnd owf·guh·fewrt*
Where's...?	**Wo ist ...?** *voh ihst ...*
the downtown area	**das Stadtzentrum** *dahs shtadt·tsehn·troom*
the bar	**die Bar** *dee bahr*
the dance club	**der Tanzclub** *dee tahnts·kloop*
Is there a cover charge?	**Kostet es Eintritt?** *kohs·tuht ehs ien·triht*

Entertainment

Can you recommend...?	**Können Sie ... empfehlen?** _kern_·uhn zee ... _ehm_·_pfeh_·luhn
a concert	**ein Konzert** _ien_·uhn kohn·_tsehrt_
a movie	**einen Film** _ien_·uhn feelm
an opera	**eine Oper** _ien_·uhn _oh_·pehr
a play	**ein Theaterstück** _ien_ teh·_ah_·tehr·shtewk
When does it start/end?	**Wann beginnt/endet es?** vahn beh·_gihnt_/_ehnd_·eht ehs
Where's ...?	**Wo ist ...?** voh ihst ...
the concert hall	**die Konzerthalle** dee kohn·_tsehrt_·hah·luh
the opera house	**das Opernhaus** dahs _oh_·pehrn·hows

YOU MAY HEAR...

Bitte schalten Sie Ihre Handys aus.
biht·tuh _shahlt_·uhn zee _eehr_·uh _hehnd_·ees ows

Turn off your mobile [cell] phones, please.

the theater	**das Theater** *dahs teh-<u>ah</u>-tehr*
the arcade	**die Spielhalle?** *dee shpeel-hah-luh*
What's the dress code?	**Wie ist die Kleiderordnung?** *vee ihst dee <u>klied</u>-ehr-ohrd-noong*
I like...	**Mir gefällt ...** *meer guh-<u>fehlt</u> ...*
classical music	**klassische Musik** *<u>klahs</u>-ihsh-uh moo-<u>zeek</u>*
folk music	**Volksmusik** *<u>fohlks</u>-moo-zeek*
jazz	**Jazz** *djehz*
pop music	**Popmusik** *<u>pohp</u>-moo-zeek*
rap	**Rap** *rehp*

For Tickets, see page 19.

Nightlife

What's there to do at night?	**Was kann man dort abends unternehmen?** *vahs kahn mahn dohrt <u>ahb</u>-uhnds oont-ehr-<u>nehm</u>-uhn*
Can you recommend...?	**Können Sie ... empfehlen?** *<u>kern</u>-uhn zee ... ehm-<u>pfeh</u>-luhn*
a bar	**eine Bar** *<u>ien</u>-uh bahr*
a cabaret	**eine Kabarettvorstellung** *ie-nuh kah-bah-reht-fohr-shteh-loong*
a casino	**ein Casino** *ien kah-<u>see</u>-noh*

Listings of regional events can be found in local newspapers.
The local tourist information office and your hotel concierge can
be useful sources of information about local events, and may also be
able to help you obtain tickets and plan transportation.

a dance club	**einen Tanzclub** _ien·uhn tahnts·kloop_
a gay club	**einen Schwulenclub** _ien·uhn shvoo·luhn·kloop_
a jazz club	**einen Jazzclub** _ien·uhn yahts·kloop_
a club with German music	**ein Club mit deutscher Musik** _ien cloob meet doyt·shuhr muh·seek_
Is there live music?	**Gibt es dort Livemusik?** _gihpt ehs dohrt liev·moo·zeek_
How do I get there?	**Wie komme ich dorthin?** _vee kohm·uh eekh dohrt·hihn_
Is there a cover charge?	**Kostet es Eintritt?** _kohs·tuht ehs ien·triht_
Let's go dancing.	**Lass uns tanzen gehen.** _ahs oons tahnt·suhn geh·uhn_
Is this area safe at night?	**Ist dieses Gebiet bei Nacht sicher?** _ihst dee·zuhs geh·beet bie nahkht zeek·hehr_

Special Requirements

Business Travel   137
Traveling with Children   140
Disabled Travelers   144

Business Travel

ESSENTIAL

I'm here on business.	**Ich bin geschäftlich hier.**
	eekh been guh·shehft·leekh heer
Here's my business card.	**Hier ist meine Visitenkarte.** *heer ihst mien·uh vih·zee·tuhn·kahr·tuh*
Can I have your card?	**Kann ich Ihre Karte haben?**
	kahn eekh ihhr·uh kahrt·uh hah·buhn
I have a meeting with...	**Ich habe ein Meeting mit ...** *eekh hahb·uh ien mee·teeng miht ...*
Where's...?	**Wo ist...?** *voh ihst*
the convention hall	**der Kongressaal** *dehr kohn·grehs·sahl*
the meeting room	**das Konferenzzimmer**
	dahs kohn·fehr·ehnts·tsihm·her

Germans are generally formal and so are their greetings.
Business introductions are always accompanied by a handshake.
Address business colleagues by title: **Herr** (Mr.), **Frau** (Miss/Ms./
Mrs.) or **Herr Dr.** (Dr.) and the person's last name. **Herr Professor** and
Frau Professor are also used, but usually without a last name.

On Business

I'm here for...	**Ich bin für ... hier.** *eekh been fuer ... heer*
a seminar	**ein Seminar** *ien zehm·ee·nahr*
a conference	**eine Konferenz** *ien·uh kohn·feh·rehnts*
a meeting	**ein Meeting** *ien mee·teeng*

My name is…	**Mein Name ist …** *mien _nahm_•uh ihst …*
May I introduce my colleague…?	**Darf ich Ihnen meinen Kollegen … vorstellen?** *dahrf eekh _eehn_•uhn mien•uhn koh•_leh_•guhn … fohr•shtehl•uhn*
Pleasure to meet you.	**Freut mich.** *froyt meekh*
I have a meeting/an appointment with…	**Ich habe ein Meeting/einen Termin mit …** *eekh hahb•uh ien mee•teeng/ien•uhn tehr•_meen_ miht …*
I'm sorry I'm late.	**Es tut mir leid, dass ich spät bin.** *ehs toot meer lied dahs eekh shpayt bihn*
I need an interpreter.	**Ich brauche einen Dolmetscher.** *eek _browkh_•uh ien•uhn dohl•meh•chehr*
You can contact me at the…Hotel.	**Sie können mich im … Hotel erreichen.** *zee _kern_•uhn meekh ihm … hoh•_tehl_ ehr•_riekh_•uhn*

YOU MAY HEAR…

Haben Sie einen Termin? *_hah_•buhn zee ien•uhn tehr•_meen_*	Do you have an appointment?
Mit wem? *meet vehm*	With whom?
Er m/Sie f ist in einem Meeting. *ehr/zee ihst ihn ien•uhm _mee_•teeng*	He/She is in a meeting.
Einen Moment, bitte. *ien•uhn moh•_mehnt_ _biht_•tuh*	One moment, please.
Nehmen Sie Platz. *_nehm_•uhn zee plats*	Have a seat.
Möchten Sie etwas zu trinken? *_merkht_•uhn zee _eht_•vahs tsoo _trihnk_•uhn*	Would you like something to drink?
Vielen Dank für Ihr Kommen. *_feel_•uhn dahnk fewr eehr _kohm_•uhn*	Thank you for coming.

I'm here until…	**Ich bin bis … hier.**	*eekh bihn bihs … heer*
I need to…	**Ich muss …**	*eekh moos …*
make a call	**telefonieren**	*tehl•eh•fohn•<u>eer</u>•uhn*
make a photocopy	**eine Kopie machen**	<u>*ien*</u>*•uh* <u>*koh*</u>*•pee•uh* <u>*mahkh*</u>*•uhn*
send an e-mail	**eine E-Mail senden**	<u>*ien*</u>*•uh* <u>*ee*</u>*•mehl* <u>*zehnd*</u>*•uhn*
send a fax	**ein Fax senden**	*ien fahx* <u>*zehnd*</u>*•uhn*
send a package (for next-day delivery)	**ein Paket schicken (per Express)**	*ien pah•*<u>*keht*</u> <u>*shihk*</u>*•uhn (pehr* <u>*ehks*</u>*•prehs)*
It was a pleasure to meet you.	**Es war schön, Sie kennenzulernen.**	*ehs vahr shern zee* <u>*keh*</u>*•nehn•tsoo•lehr•nehn*

For Communications, see page 49.

Traveling with Children

ESSENTIAL

Is there a discount for kids?	**Gibt es Ermäßigung für Kinder?** *gihpt ehs ehr·meh·see·goong fewr kihn·dehr*
Can you recommend a babysitter?	**Können Sie einen Babysitter empfehlen?** *kern·uhn zee ien·uhn beh·bee·siht·ehr ehm·pfeh·luhn*
Do you have a child's seat/highchair?	**Haben Sie einen Kindersitz/Kinderstuhl?** *hah·buhn zee ien·uhn kihnd·ehr·zihts/ kihnd·ehr·shtoohl*
Where can I change the baby?	**Wo kann ich das Baby wickeln?** *voh kahn eekh dahs beh·bee vihk·uhln*

Out & About

Can you recommend something for kids?	**Können Sie etwas für Kinder empfehlen?** _kern•uhn zee eht•vahs fewr kihnd•ehr ehm•pfeh•luhn_
Where's...?	**Wo ist ...?** _voh ihst ..._
the amusement park	**der Vergnügungspark** _dehr fehrg•new•goongs•pahrk_
the arcade	**die Spielhalle?** _dee shpeel•hah•luh_
the kiddie [paddling] pool	**das Kinderbecken** _dahs kihnd•ehr•beh•kuhn_
the park	**der Park** _dehr pahrk_
the playground	**der Spielplatz** _dehr shpeel•plats_
the zoo	**der Zoo** _dehr tsoh_
Are kids allowed?	**Sind Kinder erlaubt?** _zihnt kihnd•ehr ehr•lowbt_
Is it safe for kids?	**Ist es für Kinder geeignet?** _ihst ehs fewr kihnd•ehr guh•ieg•nuht_
Is it suitable for... year olds?	**Ist es für ... Jahre alte Kinder geeignet?** _ihst ehs fewr ... yah•ruh ahlt•uh kihnd•ehr guh•ieg•nuht_

For Numbers, see page 165.

YOU MAY HEAR...

Wie süß! _vee zews_	How cute!
Wie heißt er _m_ /sie _f_ ? _vee hiest ehr/zee_	What's his/her name?
Wie alt ist er _m_ /sie _f_ ? _vee ahlt ihst ehr/zee_	How old is he/she?

Baby Essentials

Do you have . . .?	**Haben Sie . . .?** _hah_•buhn zee . . .
a baby bottle	**eine Babyflasche** _ien_•uh beh•bee•_flahsh_•uh
baby food	**Babynahrung** _beh_•bee•nahr•oong
baby wipes	**feuchte Babytücher** _foykh_•tuh _beh_•bee•tewkh•ehr
a car seat	**einen Kindersitz** _ien_•uhn _kihnd_•ehr•zihts
a children's menu/	**ein Kindermenü/eine Kinderportion**
portion	_ien_•uhn _kihnd_•ehr•meh•new/_ien_•uh
	kihnd•ehr•pohrtz•yohn•uhn
a child's seat/	**einen Kindersitz/Kinderstuhl**
highchair	_ien_•uhn _kihnd_•ehr•zihts/_kihnd_•ehr•shtoohl
a crib/cot	**ein Gitterbett/Kinderbett**
	ien giht•tehr•beht/_kihnd_•ehr•beht
diapers [nappies]	**Windeln** _vihnd_•uhln
formula [baby food]	**Babynahrung** _beh_•bee•nah•roong
a pacifier [dummy]	**einen Schnuller** _ien_•uhn _shnool_•ehr
a playpen	**einen Laufstall** _ien_•uhn _lowf_•shtahl
a stroller	**einen Kinderwagen** _ien_•uhn
[pushchair]	_kihnd_•ehr•vahg•uhn
Can I breastfeed	**Kann ich das Baby hier stillen?** _kahn_ eekh
the baby here?	dahs _beh_•bee heer _shtihl_•uhn
Where can I	**Wo kann ich das Baby stillen/wickeln?**
breastfeed/change	voh kahn eekh dahs _beh_•bee _shtihl_•uhn/_vihk_•uhln
the baby?	

For Dining with Children, see page 65.

Babysitting

Can you recommend	**Können Sie einen Babysitter empfehlen?**
a babysitter?	_kern_•uhn zee _ien_•uhn _beh_•bee•siht•ehr ehm•_pfeh_•luhn
What is the cost?	**Was sind die Kosten?** vahs zihnt dee _kohs_•tuhn

I'll be back by...	**Ich bin um ... zurück.** *eekh been oom ... tsoo•<u>rewk</u>*
If you need to	**Ich bin unter ... zu erreichen.**
contact me, call...	*eekh been <u>oont</u>•ehr ... tsoo ehr•<u>riekh</u>•uhn*

For Time, see page 166

Health & Emergency

Can you recommend	**Können Sie einen Kinderarzt empfehlen?**
a pediatrician?	*<u>kern</u>•uhn zee <u>ien</u>•uhn <u>kihnd</u>•ehr•ahrtst ehm•<u>pfeh</u>•luhn*
My child is	**Mein Kind ist allergisch auf ...**
allergic to...	*mien kihnt ihst ah•<u>lehrg</u>•eesh owf ...*
My child is missing.	**Mein Kind ist weg.** *mien kihnt ihst vehk*
Have you seen	**Haben Sie einen Jungen/ein Mädchen gesehen?**
a boy/girl?	*<u>hah</u>•buhn zee <u>ien</u>•uhn <u>yoong</u>•uhn/ien <u>meht</u>•khuhn guh•<u>zeh</u>•uhn*

For Meals & Cooking, see page 67.

For Health, see page 150.

For Police, see page 148.

Disabled Travelers

ESSENTIAL

Is there…?	**Gibt es …?** *gihpt ehs …*
access for the disabled	**einen Zugang für Behinderte** *ien•uhn tsoo•gahng fewr beh•hihnd•ehrt•uh*
a wheelchair ramp	**eine Rollstuhlrampe** *ien•uh rohl•shtool•rahm•puh*
a disabled-accessible toilet	**eine Behindertentoilette** *ien•uh beh•hihn•dehrt•uhn•toy•leh•tuh*
I need…	**Ich brauche …** *eekh browkh•uh …*
assistance	**Hilfe** *hihlf•uh*
an elevator [a lift]	**einen Fahrstuhl** *ien•uhn fahr•shtoohl*
a ground-floor room	**ein Zimmer im Erdgeschoss** *ien tsihm•ehr ihm ehrd•guh•shohs*

Asking for Assistance

I'm...	**Ich bin ...** *eekh bihn ...*
disabled	**behindert** *beh·hihn·dehrt*
visually impaired	**sehbehindert** *zeh·buh·hihn·dehrt*
hearing impaired/ deaf	**hörgeschädigt/taub** *her·guh·sheh·deegt/towb*
I'm unable to walk far/use the stairs.	**Ich kann nicht weit laufen/die Treppe benutzen.** *eekh kahn neekht viet low·fuhn/dee trehp·uh beh·noot·suhn*
Please speak louder.	**Bitte sprechen Sie lauter.** *biht·tuh shprehkh·uhn zee lowt·ehr*
Can I bring my wheelchair?	**Kann ich meinen Rollstuhl mitbringen?** *kahn eekh mien·uhn rohl·shtoohl miht·brihng·uhn*
Are guide dogs permitted?	**Sind Blindenhunde erlaubt?** *zihnt blihnd·uhn·hoond·uh ehr·lowbt*
Can you help me?	**Können Sie mir helfen?** *kern·uhn zee meer hehlf·uhn*
Please open/hold the door.	**Bitte öffnen/halten Sie die Tür.** *biht·tuh erf·nuhn/hahlt·uhn zee dee tewr*

In an Emergency

Emergencies	147
Police	148
Health	150
The Basics	159

Emergencies

ESSENTIAL

Help!	**Hilfe!** _hihlf·uh_
Go away!	**Gehen Sie weg!** _geh·uhn zee vehk_
Stop, thief!	**Haltet den Dieb!** _hahlt·uht dehn deeb_
Get a doctor!	**Holen Sie einen Arzt!** _hohl·uhn zee ien·uhn ahrtst_
Fire!	**Feuer!** _foy·ehr_
I'm lost.	**Ich habe mich verlaufen.**
	eekh hahb·uh meekh fehr·lowf·uhn
Can you help me?	**Können Sie mir helfen?** _kern·uhn zee_
	meer hehlf·uhn

YOU MAY HEAR...

Füllen Sie dieses Formular aus.
fewl·uhn zee deez·uhs fohr·moo·lahr ows

Fill out this form.

Ihren Ausweis, bitte.
eehr·uhn ows·vies biht·tuh

Your ID, please.

Wann/Wo ist es passiert?
vahn/voh ihst ehs pah·seert

When/Where did it happen?

Wie sah er _m_/sie _f_ aus?
vee zah ehr/zee ows

What does he/she look like?

Police

ESSENTIAL

Call the police!	**Rufen Sie die Polizei!** _roof_•uhn zee dee poh•leet•_sie_
Where's the police station?	**Wo ist das Polizeirevier?** voh ihst dahs poh•leet•_sie_•ruh•veer
There was an accident/attack.	**Es gab einen Unfall/Überfall.** ehs gahb _ien_•uhn _oon_•fahl/_ewb_•ehr•fahl
My child is missing.	**Mein Kind ist weg.** mien kihnt ihst vehk
I need an interpreter.	**Ich brauche einen Dolmetscher.** eekh _browkh_•uh _ien_•uhn _dohl_•mech•ehr
I need to contact my lawyer/make a phone call.	**Ich muss mit meinem Anwalt sprechen/ telefonieren.** eekh moos miht _mien_•uhm _ahn_•vahlt _shpreh_•khehn/tehl•eh•fohn•_eer_•uhn
I'm innocent.	**Ich bin unschuldig.** eekh bihn _oon_•shoold•eekh

---

In an emergency, dial: **110** for the police
112 for the fire brigade
115 for the ambulance

Crime & Lost Property

I'd like to report...	**Ich möchte ... melden.** eekh _merkht_•uh ... _mehld_•uhn
a mugging	**einen Überfall** _ien_•uhn _ewb_•ehr•fahl
a rape	**eine Vergewaltigung** _ien_•uh fehr•guh•_vahlt_•ee•goong
a theft	**einen Diebstahl** _ien_•uhn _deeb_•shtahl

I've been mugged	**Ich wurde überfallen**
	eekh <u>voor</u>•duh ewb•ehr•<u>fahl</u>•uhn
I've been robbed	**Ich wurde beraubt** *eekh <u>voor</u>•duh beh•<u>rowbt</u>*
I've lost…	**Ich habe … verloren.**
	eekh <u>hahb</u>•uh … fehr•<u>lohr</u>•uhn
…was stolen.	**… wurde gestohlen.** … <u>voor</u>•duh
	geh•<u>shtohl</u>•uhn
My backpack	**Mein Rucksack** *mien <u>rook</u>•zahk*
My bicycle	**Mein Fahrrad** *mien <u>fahr</u>•ahd*
My camera	**Meine Kamera** *<u>mien</u>•uh <u>kah</u>•meh•rah*
My (hire) car	**Mein Mietauto** *mien <u>meet</u>•ow•toh*
My computer	**Mein Computer** *mien kohm•<u>pjoo</u>•tehr*
My credit card	**Meine Kreditkarte** *<u>mien</u>•uh kreh•<u>deet</u>•kahrt•uh*
My jewelry	**Mein Schmuck** *mien shmook*
My money	**Mein Geld** *mien gehlt*
My passport	**Mein Reisepass** *mien <u>riez</u>•uh•pahs*
My purse [handbag]	**Meine Handtasche** *<u>mien</u>•uh <u>hahnd</u>•tahsh•uh*
My traveler's checks [cheques]	**Meine Reisechecks** *<u>mien</u>•uh <u>riez</u>•uh•shehks*
My wallet	**Meine Brieftasche** *<u>mien</u>•uh <u>breef</u>•tahsh•uh*

| I need a police report. | **Ich brauche einen Polizeibericht.** *eekh browkh•uh ien•uhn poh•leet•sie•beh•reekht* |
| Where is the British/American/Irish embassy? | **Wo ist die britische/amerikanische/irische Botschaft?** *voh ihst dee brih•tih•shuh/ah•meh•rih•kah•nih•shuh/eer•ih•shuh boht•shaft* |

Health

ESSENTIAL

I'm sick.	**Ich bin krank.** *eekh bihn krahnk*
I need an English-speaking doctor.	**Ich brauche einen englischsprechenden Arzt.** *eekh browkh•uh ien•uhn ehng•glihsh•shprehkh•ehnd•uhn ahrtst*
It hurts here.	**Es tut hier weh.** *ehs toot heer veh*
I have a stomachache.	**Ich habe Magenschmerzen.** *eekh hahb•uh mahg•uhn•shmehrt•suhn*

Finding a Doctor

Can you recommend a doctor/dentist?	**Können Sie einen Arzt/Zahnarzt empfehlen?** *kern•uhn zee ien•uhn ahrtst/tsahn•ahrtst ehm•pfeh•luhn*
Can the doctor come here?	**Kann der Arzt herkommen?** *kahn dehr ahrtst hehr•kohm•uhn*
I need an English-speaking doctor.	**Ich brauche einen englischsprechenden Arzt.** *eekh browkh•uh ien•uhn ehng•gleesh•shprehkh•ehnd•uhn ahrtst*
What are the office hours?	**Wann sind die Sprechstunden?** *vahn zihnt dee shprekh•shtoond•uhn*
It's urgent.	**Es ist dringend.** *ehs ihst dreeng•uhnt*

I'd like an appointment for...	**Ich möchte einen Termin für ...** *eekh merkht•uh ien•uhn tehr•meen fewr ...*
today	**heute** *hoy•tuh*
tomorrow	**morgen** *mohr•guhn*
as soon as possible	**so bald wie möglich** *zoh bahld vee merg•leekh*

Symptoms

I'm bleeding.	**Ich blute.** *eekh bloot•uh*
I'm constipated.	**Ich habe Verstopfung.** *eekh hahb•uh fehr•shtohpf•oong*
I'm dizzy.	**Mir ist schwindlig.** *meer ihst shvihnd•leek*
I'm nauseous.	**Mir ist schlecht.** *meer ihst shlehkht*
I'm vomiting.	**Ich übergebe mich.** *eekh ewb•ehr•gehb•uh meekh*
It hurts here.	**Es tut hier weh.** *ehs toot heer veh*
I have...	**Ich habe ...** *eekh hahb•uh ...*
an allergic reaction	**eine allergische Reaktion** *ien•uh ah•lehr•geesh•uh reh•ahk•syon*
chest pain	**Brustschmerzen** *broost•shmehrt•suhn*
cramps	**Krämpfe** *krehmp•fuh*
diarrhea	**Durchfall** *doorkh•fahl*
an earache	**Ohrenschmerzen** *oht•uhn•shmehrt•suhn*
a fever	**Fieber** *feeb•ehr*
pain	**Schmerzen** *shmehrt•suhn*
a rash	**einen Ausschlag** *ien•uhn ows•shlahg*
a sprain	**eine Verstauchung** *ien•uh fehr•shtowkh•oong*
some swelling	**eine Schwellung** *ien•uh shvehl•oong*
a sore throat	**Halsschmerzen** *hahls•shmehrt•suhn*
a stomachache	**Magenschmerzen** *mahg•uhn•shmehrt•suhn*
sunstroke	**einen Sonnenstich** *ien•uhn zohn•uhn•shteekh*
I've been sick [ill] for...days.	**Ich bin seit ... Tagen krank.** *eekh bihn ziet ... tahg•uhn krahnk*

YOU MAY HEAR...

Was stimmt nicht mit Ihnen?
vahs shtihmt neekht miht eehn-uhn

Wo tut es weh? *voh toot ehs veh*

Tut es hier weh? *toot ehs heer veh*

Nehmen Sie Medikamente?
nehm-uhn zee mehd-ee-kah-mehnt-uh

Sind Sie auf irgendetwas allergisch?
zihnt zee owf eer-guhnd-eht-vahs ah-lehr-geesh

Öffnen Sie Ihren Mund.
erf-nuhn zee eehr-uhn moont

Tief einatmen. *teef ien-aht-muhn*

Bitte husten. *biht-tuh hoos-tuhn*

Gehen Sie ins Krankenhaus.
geh-uhn zee ihns krahnk-uhn-hows

Es ist ... *ehs ihst ...*

    gebrochen *geh-brohkh-uhn*

    ansteckend *ahn-shtehk-uhnt*

    infiziert *een-fee-tseert*

    verstaucht *fehr-shtowkht*

    nichts Ernstes *neekhts ehrnst-uhs*

What's wrong?

Where does it hurt?
Does it hurt here?
Are you on
medication?
Are you allergic to
anything?
Open your mouth.

Breathe deeply.
Cough, please.
Go to the hospital.

It's...
broken
contagious
infected
sprained
nothing serious

Conditions

I'm...	**Ich bin ...** *eekh bihn ...*
anemic	**anämisch** *ah-nay-meesh*
asthmatic	**Asthmatiker** *ahst-maht-eek-ehr*
diabetic	**Diabetiker** *dee-ah-beht-eek-her*
epileptic	**Epileptiker/Epileptikerin** *eh-pih-lehp-tih-kuhr/ eh-pih-lehp-tih-kuh-rihn*

I'm allergic to antibiotics/penicillin.	**Ich bin allergisch auf Antibiotika/Penicillin.** *eekh bihn ah·lehrg·eesh owf ahn·tee·bee·oh·tee·kah/ peh·nih·sihl·ihn*
I have...	**Ich habe ...** *eekh hahb·uh ...*
arthritis	**Arthritis** *ahr·tree·tihs*
a heart condition	**eine Herzkrankheit** *ien·uh hehrts·krahnk·hiet*
high/low blood pressure	**hohen/niedrigen Blutdruck** *hoh·uhn/ need·ree·gehn bloot·drook*
I'm on...	**Ich nehme ...** *eekh nehm·uh ...*

For Meals & Cooking, see page 67.

Treatment

Do I need a prescription/ medicine?	**Brauche ich ein Rezept/Medikament?** *browkh·uh eekh ien reh·tsehpt/mehd·ee·kah·mehnt*
Can you prescribe a generic drug? [unbranded medication]	**Können Sie ein ähnliches, günstiges Medikament verschreiben?** *kern·uhn zee ien ehn·lee·khehs gewn·stee·guhs meh·dee·kah·mehnt fehr·shrieb·uhn*
Where can I get it?	**Wo kann ich es bekommen?** *voh kahn eekh ehs buh·kohm·uhn*
Is this over the counter?	**Ist es rezeptfrei?** *ihst ehs reh·tsehpt·frie*

For What to Take, see page 156.

Hospital

Notify my family, please.	**Bitte benachrichtigen Sie meine Familie.** *biht·tuh buh·nahkh·reekh·tih·guhn zee mien·uh fah·mee·lee·uh*
I'm in pain.	**Ich habe Schmerzen.** *eekh hahb·uh shmehrt·suhn*
I need a doctor/nurse.	**Ich brauche einen Arzt/eine Schwester.** *eekh browkh·uh ien·uhn ahrtst/ien·uh shvehs·tehr*

| When are visiting hours? | **Wann ist die Besuchszeit?** *vahn ihst dee beh-zookhs-tsiet* |
| I'm visiting... | **Ich besuche ...** *eekh beh-zookh-uh ...* |

Dentist

I have...	**Ich habe ...** *eekh hahb-uh ...*
a broken tooth	**einen kaputten Zahn** *ien-uhn kah-poot-uhn tsahn*
a lost filling	**eine Füllung verloren** *ien-uh fewl-oong fehr-lohr-uhn*
a toothache	**Zahnschmerzen** *tsahn-shmehrts-uhn*
Can you fix this denture?	**Können Sie diese Prothese reparieren?** *kern-uhn zee deez-uh proh-teh-zuh reh-pah-reer-uhn*

Gynecologist

I have cramps/ a vaginal infection.	**Ich habe Krämpfe/eine Scheideninfektion.** *eekh hahb-uh krehmp-fuh/ ie-nuh shnied-uhn-ihn-fehk-tyohn*
I missed my period.	**Meine Periode ist ausgeblieben.** *mien-uh pehr-yoh-duh ihst ows-geh-bleeb-uhn*
I'm on the Pill.	**Ich nehme die Pille.** *eekh nehm-uh dee pihl-uh*
I'm (one/two/three/ four/five/six/seven/ eight/nine months) pregnant	**Ich bin (im ersten/zweiten/dritten/vierten/ fünften/sechsten/siebten/achten/neunten Monat) schwanger.** *eekh bihn (ihm ehrs-thun/ tsvai-thun/dree-thun/feer-thun/ewnf-thun/sehks-thun/ seeb-thun/ahkh-thun/noyn-thun moh-naht) shvahn-guhr*
I'm not pregnant.	**Ich bin nicht schwanger.** *eekh bihn (neekht) shvahng-ehr*
My last period was...	**Meine letzte Periode war ...** *mien-uh lehts-uh pehr-yohd-uh vahr ...*

Optician

I've lost…	**Ich habe … verloren.** *eekh hahb·uh …* *fehr·lohr·uhn*
a contact lens	**eine Kontaktlinse** *ien·uh kohn·tahkt·lihnz·uh*
my glasses	**meine Brille** *mien·uh brihl·uh*
a lens	**ein Brillenglas** *ien brihl·uhn·glahs*

Payment & Insurance

How much?	**Wie viel kostet es?** *vee feel kohs·tuht ehs*
Can I pay by credit card?	**Kann ich mit Kreditkarte bezahlen?** *kahn eekh miht kreh·deet·kahr·tuh beht·sahl·uhn*
I have insurance.	**Ich bin versichert.** *eekh bihn fehr·zeekh·ehrt*
I need a receipt for my insurance.	**Ich brauche eine Quittung für meine Versicherung.** *eekh browkh·uh ien·uh kviht·oong fewr mien·uh fehr·zeekh·ehr·oong*

Pharmacy

ESSENTIAL

Where's the pharmacy?	**Wo ist die Apotheke?** *voh ihst dee ah·poh·tehk·uh*
What time does it open/close?	**Wann öffnet/schließt sie?** *vahn erf·nuht/ shleest zee*
What would you recommend for…?	**Was empfehlen Sie bei …?** *vahs ehm·pfeh·luhn zee bie …*
How much do I take?	**Wie viel muss ich einnehmen?** *vee feel moos eekh ei·nehm·uhn*

What to Take

How much do I take?	**Wie viel muss ich einnehmen?**
	vee feel moos eekh ien•nehm•uhn
How often?	**Wie oft?** *vee ohft*
Is it safe for children?	**Ist es für Kinder geeignet?**
	ihst ehs fewr kihnd•ehr geh•ieg•nuht
I'm taking...	**Ich nehme ...** *eekh neh•muh ...*

In Germany, there is a distinction between **Apotheke** (pharmacy) and **Drogerie** (drugstore).
Die Apotheke, usually featuring a large red A sign, dispenses prescription and over-the-counter medication.
Die Drogerie sells toiletries and other personal items. Pharmacies are open 9:00 a.m. to 6:30 p.m. Monday to Friday, and from 9:00 a.m. to 1:00 p.m. (sometimes 4:00 p.m) on Saturday. Most large cities and towns have at least one 24-hour pharmacy. Closed pharmacies will have a sign on the door indicating the nearest 24-hour location.

YOU MAY SEE...

EINMAL/DREIMAL AM TAG	once/three times a day
TABLETTE	tablet
TROPFEN	drop
TEELÖFFEL	teaspoon
NACH/VOR/MIT DEN MAHLZEITEN	after/before/with meals
AUF LEEREN MAGEN	on an empty stomach
IM GANZEN SCHLUCKEN	swallow whole
KANN BENOMMENHEIT VERURSACHEN	may cause drowsiness
NUR ZÜR ÄUSSEREN ANWENDUNG	for external use only

Are there side effects?	**Gibt es Nebenwirkungen?** *gihpt ehs nehb•uhn•veerk•oong•uhn*
I need something for...	**Ich brauche etwas gegen ...** *ihkh browkh•uh eht•vahs geh•guhn ...*
a cold	**eine Erkältung** *ien•uh ehr•kehlt•oong*
a cough	**Husten** *hoos•tuhn*
diarrhea	**Durchfall** *doorkh•fahl*
a headache	**Kopfschmerzen** *kohpf•shmehr•tsuhn*
insect bites	**Insektenstiche** *een•zehkt•uhn•shteekh•uh*
motion [travel] sickness	**die Reisekrankheit** *dee riez•uh•krahnk•hiet*
a sore throat	**Halsschmerzen** *hahls•shmehrt•suhn*
sunburn	**Sonnenbrand** *zohn•uhn•brahnt*
a toothache	**Zahnschmerzen** *tsahn•shmehr•tsuhn*
an upset stomach	**eine Magenverstimmung** *ien•uh mahg•uhn•fehr•shtihm•oong*

Basic Supplies

I'd like…	**Ich hätte gern …** eekh <u>heh</u>·tuh gehrn …
acetaminophen [paracetamol]	**Paracetamol** pah·rah·<u>seht</u>·ah·mohl
antiseptic cream	**eine antiseptische Creme** ahn·tee·<u>zehp</u>·tee·shuh krehm
aspirin	**Aspirin** ahs·pih·<u>reen</u>
bandages	**Pflaster** <u>pflahs</u>·tehr
a comb	**einen Kamm** <u>ien</u>·uhn kahm
condoms	**Kondome** kohn·<u>dohm</u>·uh
contact lens solution	**Kontaktlinsenlösung** kohn·<u>tahkt</u>·lehnz·uhn·lerz·oong
deodorant	**Deodorant** deh·oh·doh·<u>rahnt</u>
a hairbrush	**eine Haarbürste** <u>ien</u>·uh hahr·bewr·stuh
hairspray	**Haarspray** <u>hahr</u>·shpraye
ibuprofen	**Ibuprofen** ee·boo·proh·<u>fuhn</u>
insect repellent	**Insektenspray** ihn·<u>zehkt</u>·uhn·shpray
lotion	**Lotion** loht·<u>syohn</u>
a nail file	**eine Nagelfeile** <u>ien</u>·uh <u>nahg</u>·ehl·fie·luh
a (disposable) razor	**(Wegwerf-) Rasierer** <u>vehk</u>·vehrf rah·<u>zeer</u>·ehr
razor blades	**Rasierklingen** rah·<u>zeer</u>·kleeng·uhn
rubbing alcohol [surgical spirit]	**Franzbranntwein** <u>frahnts</u>·brahnt·vien
sanitary napkins [towels]	**Monatsbinden** <u>moh</u>·nahts·bihnd·uhn
shampoo/ conditioner	**Shampoo/Spülung** <u>shahm</u>·poo/<u>shpewl</u>·oong
soap	**Seife** <u>zie</u>·fuh
sunscreen	**Sonnenmilch** <u>zohn</u>·nuhn·mihlkh
tampons	**Tampons** <u>tahm</u>·pohns

tissues	**Taschentücher** _tahsh_•uhn•tewkh•ehr	
toilet paper	**Toilettenpapier** toy•_leht_•uhn•pah•peer	
toothpaste	**Zahnpasta** _tsahn_•pahs•tah	

For Baby Essentials, see page 142.

The Basics

Grammar

Regular Verbs

Regular verbs in German are conjugated as in the table below. Note that the past is expressed with **haben** (to have) or **sein** (to be) plus the past participle. The future is formed with **werden** (will) plus the infinitive.

BEZAHLEN (to pay)		Present	Past	Future
I	**ich**	bezahl**e**	habe bezahlt	werde bezahlen
you (inf.)	**du**	bezahl**st**	hast bezahlt	wirst bezahlen
he/she/it	**er/sie/es**	bezahl**t**	hat bezahlt	wird bezahlen
we	**wir**	bezahl**en**	haben bezahlt	werden bezahlen
you (pl.) (inf.)	**ihr**	bezahl**t**	habt bezahlt	werdet bezahlen
they/you	**sie/Sie**	bezahl**en**	haben bezahlt	werden bezahlen

Example: **Ich bezahle bar.** I'll pay in cash.
Er m **/sie** f **bezahlt mit Kreditkarte.** He/She will pay with credit card.

MACHEN (to do, make)		Present	Past	Future
I	**ich**	mach**e**	habe gemacht	werde machen
you (inf.)	**du**	mach**st**	hast gemacht	wirst machen
he/she/it	**er/sie/es**	mach**t**	hat gemacht	wird machen
we	**wir**	mach**en**	haben gemacht	werden machen
you (pl.) (inf.)	**ihr**	mach**t**	habt gemacht	werdet machen
they/you	**sie/Sie**	mach**en**	haben gemacht	werden machen

Examples: **Ich mache hier Urlaub.** I'm here on vacation.
Was machen Sie beruflich? What do you do (for work)?

Irregular Verbs

There are a number of irregular verbs in German. Two common irregular verbs in German are **haben** (to have) and **sein** (to be). Conjugations follow:

HABEN (to have)		Present	Past	Future
I	**ich**	hab**e**	habe gehabt	werde haben
you (inf.)	**du**	ha**st**	hast gehabt	wirst haben
he/she/it	**er/sie/es**	ha**t**	hat gehabt	wird haben
we	**wir**	hab**en**	haben gehabt	werden haben
you (pl.) (inf.)	**ihr**	hab**t**	habt gehabt	werdet haben
they/you	**sie/Sie**	hab**en**	haben gehabt	werden haben

Example: **Ich habe einen Koffer.** I have one suitcase.
Ihr habt viel zu tun. You guys have a lot to do.

SEIN (to be)		Present	Past	Future
I	**ich**	bin	bin gewesen	werde sein
you (inf.)	**du**	bist	bist gewesen	wirst sein
he/she/it	**er/sie/es**	ist	ist gewesen	wird sein
we	**wir**	sind	sind gewesen	werden sein
you (pl.) (inf.)	**ihr**	seid	seid gewesen	werdet sein
they/you	**sie/Sie**	sind	sind gewesen	werden sein

Example: **Ich bin geschäftlich hier.** I am here on business.
Wir sind glücklich. We are happy.

Word Order

German is similar to English in terms of word order for simple sentences; it follows the subject-verb-object pattern.

Example: **Wir lassen unser Gepäck hier.** We leave our luggage here.

When the sentence doesn't begin with a subject, the word order changes: the verb and the subject are inverted.

Examples:

	Er	**ist**	**in Berlin.**		He is in Berlin.
Heute	**ist**	**er**	**in Berlin.**		Today he is in Berlin.
	Wir	**sind**	**in Berlin**	**gewesen.**	We were in Berlin.

To ask a question, begin with the verb and follow with the subject, as in English. Example: **Seid ihr in Köln gewesen?** Have you been to Cologne? (Literally: Have you to Cologne been?)

Negation

The negative is formed by putting **nicht** after the verb.

Example: **Ich bin Thomas**. I am Thomas.

Ich bin nicht Thomas. I am not Thomas.

If a noun is used, the negation is made by adding **kein** (masculine and neuter), or **keine** (feminine). For plural nouns, always add **keine**.

Example: **Wir haben keine Einzelzimmer.** We don't have any single rooms.

Imperatives

Whereas in English the imperative always looks like the infinitive ('Go!'), in German it is derived from the **du-/Sie-** form of the present tense. In the **du-** form, the **-st** is dropped. All other forms are identical to the present tense. The verb always comes first in commands.

		Go!
du	you (inf.)	**Geh!**
ihr	you (pl.) (inf.)	**Geht!**
Sie	you	**Gehen Sie!**
wir	we	**Gehen wir!** (Let's go!)

Nouns & Articles

In German, all nouns are capitalized. German nouns are also gender-specific; they can be masculine, feminine or neuter. There is no easy way to determine whether a noun is masculine, feminine or neuter.

There are three definite articles (the) in German: **der**, **die** and **das**. Masculine words use **der**, feminine words use **die** and neuter words use **das**. The only way to tell whether a word is masculine, feminine or neuter is to look at the article. For this reason, it is best to memorize the article when learning the word. For plural nouns using a definite article, all genders use **die**.

Definite examples: **der Mann** (the man), **die Männer** (the men); **die Frau** (the woman), **die Frauen** (the women); **das Kind** (neuter) (the child), **die Kinder** (neuter) (the children)

There are four cases in German. The definite articles are as follows:

	masculine	feminine	neuter	plural (all genders)
nominative	**der**	**die**	**das**	**die**
accusative	**den**	**die**	**das**	**die**
dative	**dem**	**der**	**dem**	**den**
genitive	**des**	**der**	**des**	**der**

German uses two indefinite articles (a/an): **ein** and **eine**. Masculine and neuter nouns use **ein**, and feminine nouns use **eine**. For plural nouns, the indefinite article is dropped, as in English.

Indefinite examples: **ein Zug** (a train), **Züge** (trains); **eine Karte** (a map), **Karten** (maps)

Adjectives

Adjectives must agree with the nouns they modify. Adjective endings change based on the article used and the case. For masculine nouns, **–er** is added to the adjective after an indefinite article and **–e** is added after a definite article.

Example: **ein klein<u>er</u> Herr** a short gentleman
der klein<u>e</u> Herr the short gentleman

For feminine nouns, **–e** is added to the adjective after both an indefinite and a definite article.

Example: **eine klug<u>e</u> Frau** an intelligent woman
die klug<u>e</u> Frau the intelligent woman

For neuter nouns, **–es** is added to the adjective after an indefinite article, while **–e** is added to the adjective after a definite article.

Example: **ein groß<u>es</u> Land** a big country
das groß<u>e</u> Land the big country

Comparatives & Superlatives

In German, the comparative of an adjective is usually formed by adding **–er** to the end of the adjective.

Examples: **klein** (small), **kleiner** (smaller); **billig** (cheap), **billiger** (cheaper); **groß** (big), **größer** (bigger)

The superlative is formed by adding **–sten** or **–esten** to the end of the adjective. If the adjective has a vowel of **a**, **o** or **u**, it may change to **ä**, **ö** or **ü** in the comparative and superlative forms.

Examples: **klein** (small), **klei<u>n</u>sten** (smallest); **billig** (cheap), **billigsten** (cheapest); **groß** (big); **größten** (biggest)

Possessive Adjectives

Possessive adjectives must agree in gender and number with the noun they are associated with.

| | singular | | |
	masculine/neuter	feminine	plural
my	**mein**	**meine**	**meine**
your (inf.)	**dein**	**deine**	**deine**
his/its	**sein**	**seine**	**seine**
her/their	**ihr**	**ihre**	**ihre**
your (pl.) (inf.)	**Ihr**	**Ihre**	**Ihre**
our	**unser**	**unsere**	**unsere**

Example: **Wir lassen unser Gepäck im Hotel.** We leave our luggage in the hotel.

Possessive Pronouns

Possessive pronouns agree in gender and number with the noun they replace.

	Masculine	Feminine	Neuter
mine	**meiner**	**meine**	**meines**
yours (inf.)	**deiner**	**deine**	**deines**
his/its	**seiner**	**seine**	**seines**
hers/theirs	**ihrer**	**ihre**	**ihres**
ours	**unserer**	**unsere**	**unseres**
yours (pl.) (inf.)	**eurer**	**eure**	**eures**

Example: **Wem gehört der Schlüssel?** Whose key is this?
Das ist meiner. It's mine.

Adverbs & Adverbial Expressions

In German, adverbs are usually identical to adjectives but, unlike adjectives, their endings don't change.
Examples:
Adjective: **das gute Essen** the good food
Adverb: **Sie sprechen gut Deutsch**. You speak German well.

Numbers

ESSENTIAL

0	**null**	*nool*
1	**eins**	*iens*
2	**zwei**	*tsvie*
3	**drei**	*drie*
4	**vier**	*feer*
5	**fünf**	*fewnf*
6	**sechs**	*zehks*
7	**sieben**	*<u>zeeb</u>•uhn*
8	**acht**	*ahkht*
9	**neun**	*noyn*
10	**zehn**	*tsehn*
11	**elf**	*ehlf*
12	**zwölf**	*tsverlf*
13	**dreizehn**	*<u>driet</u>•sehn*
14	**vierzehn**	*<u>feert</u>•sehn*
15	**fünfzehn**	*<u>fewnf</u>•tsehn*
16	**sechszehn**	*<u>zehk</u>•tsehn*
17	**siebzehn**	*<u>zeep</u>•tsehn*
18	**achtzehn**	*<u>ahkht</u>•tsehn*
19	**neunzehn**	*<u>noyn</u>•tsehn*
20	**zwanzig**	*<u>tsvahnt</u>•seek*
21	**einundzwanzig**	*<u>ien</u>•oond•tsvahn•tseek*
22	**zweiundzwanzig**	*<u>tsvie</u>•oond•tsvahn•tseek*
30	**dreißig**	*<u>drie</u>•seekh*
31	**einunddreißig**	*<u>ien</u>•oont•drie•seekh*
40	**vierzig**	*<u>feert</u>•seek*
50	**fünfzig**	*<u>fewnf</u>•tseeg*

60	**sechzig**	_zehkht_·seeg
70	**siebzig**	_zeeb_·tseeg
80	**achtzig**	_ahkht_·tseeg
90	**neunzig**	_noynt_·seek
100	**einhundert**	_ien_·hoon·dehrt
101	**einhunderteins**	_ien_·hoon·dehr·tiens
200	**zweihundert**	_tsvie_·hoon·dehrt
500	**fünfhundert**	_fewnf_·hoon·dehrt
1,000	**eintausend**	_ien_·tow·zuhnt
10,000	**zehntausend**	_tsehn_·tow·zuhnt
1,000,000	**eine Million**	_ien_·uh mihl·_yohn_

Ordinal Numbers

first	**erste**	_ehrs_·tuh
second	**zweite**	_tsviet_·uh
third	**dritte**	_driht_·tuh
fourth	**vierte**	_feer_·tuh
fifth	**fünfte**	_fewnf_·tuh
once	**einmal**	_ien_·mahl
twice	**zweimal**	_tsvie_·mahl
three times	**dreimal**	_drie_·mahl

Time

ESSENTIAL

What time is it?	**Wie spät ist es?** _vee shpayt ihst ehs_
It's midday.	**Es ist zwölf.** _ehs ihst tsverlf_
At midnight.	**Um Mitternacht.** _oom miht·tehr·nahkht_

From one o'clock to two o'clock.	**Von eins bis zwei.** *fohn iens bihs tsvie*
Five past three.	**Fünf nach drei.** *fewnf nahkh drie*
A quarter to four.	**Viertel vor vier.** <u>*feert*</u>*·uhl fohr feer*
5:30 a.m./5:30 p.m.	**Fünf Uhr dreißig/Siebzehn Uhr dreißig** *fewnf oohr* <u>*drie*</u>*·seeg/*<u>*zeeb*</u>*·tsuhn oohr* <u>*drie*</u>*·seeg*

Germans use the 24-hour clock in formal contexts (radio, TV, transportation schedules and digital clocks) or when confusion might otherwise arise. The morning hours from 1:00 a.m. to noon are the same as in English. After that, just add 12: so 1:00 p.m. would be 13:00, 5:00 p.m. would be 17:00 and so on. This system eliminates the necessity of 'a.m.' and 'p.m.' markers. When the 12-hour clock is used, **morgens** (in the morning) and **abends** (in the evening) are added after the number for clarity.

Days

ESSENTIAL

Monday	**Montag** <u>*mohn*</u>*·tahk*
Tuesday	**Dienstag** <u>*deens*</u>*·tahk*
Wednesday	**Mittwoch** <u>*miht*</u>*·vohkh*
Thursday	**Donnerstag** <u>*dohn*</u>*·ehrs·tahk*
Friday	**Freitag** <u>*frie*</u>*·tahk*
Saturday	**Samstag** <u>*zahms*</u>*·tahk*
Sunday	**Sonntag** *zohn·tahk*

Dates

yesterday	**gestern** _gehs_•tehrn
today	**heute** _hoy_•tuh
tomorrow	**morgen** _mohr_•guhn
day	**Tag** _tahk_
week	**Woche** _vohkh_•uh
month	**Monat** _moh_•naht
year	**Jahr** _yahr_

German calendars and weeks, like the U.K., are arranged
Monday through Sunday (in contrast to the U.S., where calendars
run Sunday through Saturday).

Months

January	**Januar** _yahn_•wahr
February	**Februar** _fehb_•rooahr
March	**März** _mehrts_
April	**April** _ah_•_prihl_
May	**Mai** _mie_

June	**Juni** _yoo_•nee
July	**Juli** _yoo_•lee
August	**August** _ow_•goost
September	**September** zehp•_tehm_•behr
October	**Oktober** ohk•_toh_•behr
November	**November** noh•_vehm_•behr
December	**Dezember** deh•_tsehm_•behr

Germany follows a day-month-year format instead of the month-day-year format used in the U.S.
For example: July 25, 2008; 25/07/08 = 7/25/2008 in the U.S.

Seasons

in...	**im ...** ihm ...
spring	**Frühling** _frewh_•leeng
summer	**Sommer** _zohm_•ehr
fall [autumn]	**Herbst** hehrbst
winter	**Winter** _vihnt_•ehr

Holidays

January 1: New Year's Day, **Neujahrstag**
January 6: Epiphany, **Heilige Drei Könige**
May 1: Labor Day, **Tag der Arbeit**
August 15: Assumption Day, **Mariä Himmelfahrt**
October 3: German Unity Day, **Tag der Deutschen Einheit**
November 1: All Saint's Day, **Allerheiligen**
December 25: Christmas, **Erster Weihnachtstag**
December 26: St. Stephen's Day [Boxing Day], **Zweiter Weihnachtstag**

The Easter (movable) holidays are:
Ascension Day, **Christ Himmelfahrt**
Easter Sunday, **Ostersonntag**
Easter Monday, **Ostermontag**
Feast of Corpus Christi, **Fronleichnam**
Good Friday, **Karfreitag**
Pentecost, **Pfinstsonntag**
Pentecost Monday, **Pfinstmontag**

One of Germany's most famous festivals is **Oktoberfest**, held each September in Munich. This food and beer festival extends for more than two weeks and is attended by about six million visitors from around the world. Another popular festival is **Karneval**, celebrated with parades and parties the week before Lent in areas that have substantial Catholic populations. Christmas festivities and markets are also very popular in Germany. Locals and tourists alike visit these markets to purchase local handmade crafts such as toys, wooden carvings, marionettes, candles, lambskin shoes and much more. There are plenty of food vendors available with numerous tasty treats to try.

Conversion Tables

When you know	Multiply by	To find
ounces	28.3	grams
pounds	0.45	kilograms
inches	2.54	centimeters
feet	0.3	meters
miles	1.61	kilometers
square inches	6.45	sq. centimeters
square feet	0.09	sq. meters

square miles	2.59	sq. kilometers
pints (U.S./Brit)	0.47/0.56	liters
gallons (U.S./Brit)	3.8/4.5	liters
Fahrenheit	5/9, after −32	Centigrade
Centigrade	9/5, then +32	Fahrenheit

Kilometers to Miles Conversions

1 km – 0.62 mi	20 km – 12.4 mi
5 km – 3.10 mi	50 km – 31.0 mi
10 km – 6.20 mi	100 km – 61.0 mi

Measurement

1 gram	**ein Gramm** *ien grahm*	= 0.035 oz.
1 kilogram (kg)	**ein Kilogramm** *ien kee·loh·grahm*	= 2.2 lb
1 liter (l)	**ein Liter** *ien lee·tehr*	= 1.06 U.S/0.88 Brit. quarts
1 centimeter (cm)	**ein Zentimeter** *ien tsehn·tee·muh·tehr*	= 0.4 inch
1 meter (m)	**ein Meter** *ien meh·tehr*	= 39.37 inches/ 3.28 ft.
1 kilometer (km)	**ein Kilometer** *ien kee·loh·meh·tehr*	= 0.62 mile

Temperature

-40° C – -40° F	-1° C – 30° F	20° C – 68° F
-30° C – -22° F	0° C – 32° F	25° C – 77° F
-20° C – -4° F	5° C – 41° F	30° C – 86° F
-10° C – 14° F	10° C – 50° F	35° C – 95° F
-5° C – 23° F	15° C – 59° F	

Oven Temperature

100° C – 212° F	175° C – 347° F	204° C – 400° F
121° C – 250° F	177° C – 350° F	220° C – 428° F
149° C – 300° F	180° C – 356° F	250° C – 482° F
150° C – 302° F	200° C – 392° F	260° C – 500° F

Dictionary

English–German 173

German–English 199

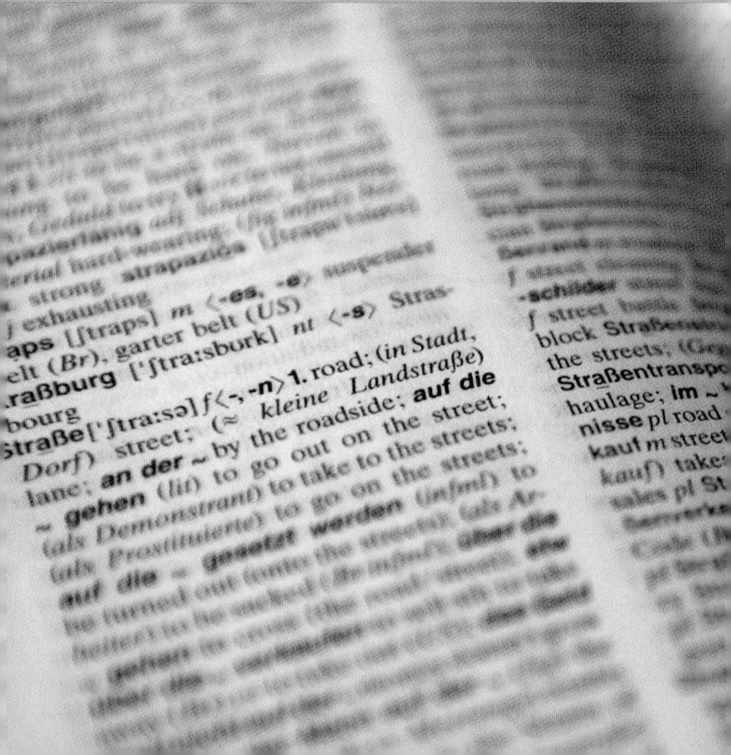

A

accept *v* akzeptieren

access *n* der Zutritt

accident der Unfall

accommodation die Unterkunft

account *n* (**bank**) das Konto

acupuncture die Akupunktur

adapter der Adapter

address *n* die Adresse

admission (price) der Eintritt

after nach;

~**noon** der Nachmittag;

~**shave** das Aftershave

age *n* das Alter

agency die Agentur

AIDS AIDS

air *n* die Luft; ~ **conditioning** die Klimaanlage; ~**-dry** lufttrocknen; ~ **pump** die Luftpumpe; ~**line** die Fluggesellschaft; ~**mail** die Luftpost; ~**plane** das Flugzeug; ~**port** der Flughafen

aisle der Gang; ~ **seat** der Platz am Gang

allergic allergisch; ~ **reaction** die allergische Reaktion

allow erlauben

alone allein

alter *v* umändern

alternate route die Alternativroute

aluminum foil die Aluminiumfolie

amazing erstaunlich

ambulance der Krankenwagen

American *adj* amerikanisch

amusement park der Vergnügungspark

anemic anämisch

anesthesia die Anästhesie

animal das Tier

ankle das Fußgelenk

antibiotic *n* das Antibiotikum

antiques store das Antiquitätengeschäft

antiseptic cream die antiseptische Creme

apartment das Apartment

appendix (body part) der Blinddarm

appetizer die Vorspeise

adj adjective	**BE** British English	**prep** preposition
adv adverb	**n** noun	**v** verb

appointment der Termin
arcade die Spielhalle
area code die Ortsvorwahl
arm n **(body part)** der Arm
aromatherapy die Aromatherapie
around (the corner) um;
~ **(price)** ungefähr
arrival Ankunft
arrive ankommen
artery die Arterie
arthritis die Arthritis
art die Kunst
Asian adj asiatisch
aspirin das Aspirin
asthmatic asthmatisch
ATM der Bankautomat;
~ **card** die Bankkarte
attack v angreifen
attraction (place)
die Sehenswürdigkeit
attractive attraktiv
Australia das Australien
Australian adj australisch
automatic automatisch;
~ **car** das Auto mit
Automatikschaltung
available verfügbar

B
baby das Baby;
~ **bottle** die Babyflasche;

~ **wipe** das Baby-Pflegetuch;
~**sitter** der Babysitter
back (body part) der Rücken;
~**ache** die Rückenschmerzen;
~**pack** der Rucksack
bag die Tasche
baggage [BE] das Gepäck;
~ **claim** die Gepäckausgabe;
~ **ticket** der Gepäckschein
bake v backen
bakery die Bäckerei
ballet das Ballett
bandage das Pflaster
bank n die Bank
bar (place) die Bar
barbecue (device) n der Grill
barber der Herrenfriseur
baseball der Baseball
basket (grocery store)
der Einkaufskorb
basketball der Basketball
bathroom das Bad
battery die Batterie
battleground das Schlachtfeld
be v sein
beach der Strand
beautiful wunderschön; ~ schön
bed n das Bett; ~ **and breakfast**
die Pension
before vor
begin beginnen

beginner der Anfänger

behind (direction) hinter

beige *adj* beige

belt der Gürtel

best *adj* beste; **~ before** mindestens haltbar bis

better besser

bicycle das Fahrrad

big groß; **~ger** größerger

bike route die Radroute

bikini der Bikini

bill *n* **(money)** der Geldschein; **~** *n* **(of sale)** die Rechnung

bird der Vogel

birthday der Geburtstag

black *adj* schwarz

bladder die Blase

bland fad

blanket die Decke

bleed bluten

blender der Mixer

blood das Blut; **~ pressure** der Blutdruck

blouse die Bluse

blue *adj* blau

board *v* einsteigen; **~ing pass** die Bordkarte

boat *n* das Boot

boil *v* kochen

bone *n* der Knochen

book *n* das Buch;

~store der Buchladen

boot *n* der Stiefel

boring langweilig

botanical garden der botanische Garten

bother *v* belästigen

bottle *n* die Flasche; **~ opener** der Flaschenöffner

bowl *n* die Schüssel

boxing match der Boxkampf

boy der Junge; **~friend** der Freund

bra der BH

bracelet das Armband

brake (car) die Bremse

breaded paniert

break *v* **(bone)** brechen

breakdown (car) die Panne

breakfast *n* das Frühstück

break-in (burglary) *n* der Einbruch

breast die Brust; **~feed** *v* stillen

breathe atmen

bridge die Brücke

briefs (clothing) der Schlüpfer

bring bringen

British *adj* britisch

broken kaputt; **~ (bone)** gebrochen

brooch die Brosche

broom der Besen

brother der Bruder

brown *adj* braun
bug (insect) *n* das Insekt
building das Gebäude
burn *v* brennen
bus *n* der Bus;
  ~ **station** der Busbahnhof;
  ~ **stop** die Bushaltestelle;
  ~ **ticket** die Busfahrkarte;
  ~ **tour** die Busreise
business *adj* Geschäfts-;
  ~ **card** die Visitenkarte;
  ~ **center** das Geschäftszentrum;
  ~ **class** die Business-Class;
  ~ **hours** die Öffnungszeiten
butcher *n* der Fleischer
buttocks der Po
buy *v* kaufen
bye auf Wiedersehen

C

cabaret das Kabarett
cable car die Seilbahn
cafe (place) das Café
call *v* **(phone)** anrufen;
  ~ *n* der Anruf ~ **collect** ein
  R-Gespräch führen
calorie die Kalorie
camera die Kamera;
  ~ **case** die Kameratasche; **digital**
  ~ die Digitalkamera
camp *v* campen; **~ing stove**

der Campingkocher; **~site** der
  Campingplatz
can opener der Dosenöffner
Canada das Kanada
Canadian *adj* kanadisch
cancel stornieren
candy die Süßigkeit
canned good die Konserve
canyon der Canyon
car das Auto;
  ~ **hire [BE]** die Autovermietung; ~
  park [BE] der Parkplatz;
  ~ **rental** die Autovermietung; ~
  seat der Autositz
carafe die Karaffe
card *n* die Karte;
  ATM ~ die Bankkarte;
  credit ~ die Kreditkarte;
  debit ~ die EC-Karte;
  phone ~ die Telefonkarte
carry-on *n* **(piece of hand
  luggage)** das Handgepäckstück
cart (grocery store) der
  Einkaufswagen; ~ **(luggage)** der
  Gepäckwagen
carton (of cigarettes) die Stange
  (Zigaretten);
  ~ **(of groceries)** die Packung
cash *n* das Bargeld;
  ~ *v* einlösen
cashier der Kassierer

casino das Casino
castle das Schloss
cathedral die Kathedrale
cave n die Höhle
CD die CD
cell phone das Handy
Celsius Celsius
centimeter der Zentimeter
certificate das Zertifikat
chair n der Stuhl;
~ **lift** der Sessellift
change v **(baby)** wickeln;
~ **(buses)** umsteigen;
~ **(money)** wechseln;
~ n **(money)** das Wechselgeld
charge v **(credit card)**
belasten; ~ **(cost)** verlangen
cheap billig; ~**er** billiger
check v **(luggage)**
aufgeben; ~ **(on something)**
prüfen; n **(payment)** der
Scheck; ~**-in** das Check-in;
~**ing account** das Girokonto;
~**-out** das Check-out
Cheers! Prost!
chemical toilet die
Campingtoilette
chemist [BE] die Apotheke
chest (body part) die Brust;
~ **pain** die Brustschmerzen
chewing gum der Kaugummi

child das Kind;
~**'s seat** der Kinderstuhl
children's menu das Kindermenü
children's portion die Kinderportion
Chinese adj chinesisch
chopsticks die Stäbchen
church die Kirche
cigar die Zigarre
cigarette die Zigarette
class n die Klasse;
business ~ die Business-Class;
economy ~ die Economy-Class;
first ~ die erste Klasse
classical music die
klassische Musik
clean v reinigen; ~ adj
(clothes) sauber; ~**ing**
product das Reinigungsmittel
clear v **(on an ATM)** löschen
cliff die Klippe
cling film [BE] die Klarsichtfolie
close v **(a shop)** schließen
closed geschlossen
clothing die Bekleidung;
~ **store** das Bekleidungsgeschäft
club n der Club
coat der Mantel
coin die Münze
colander das Sieb
cold n **(sickness)** die Erkältung; ~
adj **(temperature)** kalt

colleague der Kollege
cologne das Kölnischwasser
color *n* die Farbe
comb *n* der Kamm
come *v* kommen
complaint die Beschwerde
computer der Computer
concert das Konzert;
 ~ hall die Konzerthalle
condition (medical) die
 Beschwerden
conditioner (hair) die Spülung
condom das Kondom
conference die Konferenz
confirm bestätigen
congestion (medical) der Blutstau
connect (internet) verbinden
connection (travel/internet)
 die Verbindung; **~ flight** der
 Anschlussflug
constipated verstopft
consulate das Konsulat
consultant der Berater
contact *v* kontaktieren
contact lens die Kontaktlinse;
 ~ solution Kontaktlinsenlösung
contagious ansteckend
convention hall der Kongresssaal
conveyor belt das Förderband
cook *v* kochen
cool *adj* **(temperature)** kalt

copper *n* das Kupfer
corkscrew *n* der Korkenzieher
cost *v* kosten
cotton die Baumwolle
cough *v* husten;
 ~ *n* der Husten
country code die Landesvorwahl
cover charge der Preis pro Gedeck
cream (ointment) die Creme
credit card die Kreditkarte
crew neck der runde Halsausschnitt
crib das Kinderbett
crystal *n* **(glass)** das Kristall
cup *n* die Tasse
currency die Währung; **~ exchange**
 der Währungsumtausch; **~**
 exchange office die Wechselstube
current account [BE] das
 Girokonto
customs der Zoll
cut *v* schneiden;
 ~ *n* **(injury)** der Schnitt
cute süß
cycling das Radfahren

D

damage *v* beschädigen
dance *v* tanzen; **~ club** der
 Tanzclub; **~ing** das Tanzen
dangerous gefährlich
dark *adj* dunkel

date *n* **(calendar)** das Datum

day der Tag

deaf *adj* taub

debit card die EC-Karte

deck chair der Liegestuhl

declare *v* **(customs)** deklarieren

decline *v* **(credit card)** ablehnen

deep *adj* tief

degree (temperature) das Grad

delay *v* verzögern

delete *v* **(computer)** löschen

delicatessen das Feinkostgeschäft

delicious lecker

denim das Denim

dentist der Zahnarzt

denture die Zahnprothese

deodorant das Deodorant

department store das Kaufhaus

departure (plane) der Abflug

deposit *v* **(money)** einzahlen; ~ *n* **(bank)** die Einzahlung

desert *n* die Wüste

detergent das Waschmittel

develop *v* **(film)** entwickeln

diabetic *adj* diabetisch; *n* der Diabetiker

dial *v* wählen

diamond der Diamant

diaper die Windel

diarrhea der Durchfall

diesel der Diesel

difficult schwierig

digital digital; ~ **camera** die Digitalkamera; ~ **photo** das Digitalfoto; ~ **print** der digitale Ausdruck

dining room das Esszimmer

dinner das Abendessen

direction die Richtung

dirty schmutzig

disabled *adj* **(person)** behindert; ~ **accessible [BE]** behindertengerecht

disconnect (computer) trennen

discount *n* der Rabatt; die Ermäßigung

dishes (kitchen) das Geschirr

dishwasher der Geschirrspüler

dishwashing liquid das Geschirrspülmittel

display *n* **(device)** das Display; ~ **case** die Vitrine

disposable *n* der Einwegartikel; ~ **razor** der Einweg-Rasierer

dive *v* tauchen

diving equipment die Tauchausrüstung

divorce *v* sich scheiden lassen

dizzy *adj* schwindelig

doctor *n* der Arzt

doll *n* die Puppe

dollar (U.S.) der Dollar

domestic inländisch;
  ~ flight der Inlandsflug
door die Tür
dormitory der Schlafsaal
double bed das Doppelbett
downtown *n* das Stadtzentrum
dozen das Dutzend
drag lift der Schlepplift
dress (clothing) das Kleid;
  ~ code die Kleiderordnung
drink *v* trinken; **~** *n* das Getränk;
  ~ menu die Getränkekarte; **~ing
  water** das Trinkwasser
drive *v* fahren
driver's license number die
  Führerscheinnummer
drop *n* **(medicine)** der Tropfen
drowsiness die Schläfrigkeit
dry clean chemisch reinigen;
  ~er's die chemische Reinigung
dubbed synchronisiert
during während
duty (tax) der Zoll; **~-free** zollfrei
DVD die DVD

E

ear das Ohr; **~ache** die
  Ohrenschmerzen
earlier früher
early früh
earring der Ohrring

east *n* der Osten
easy leicht
eat *v* essen
economy class die Economy-Class
elbow *n* der Ellenbogen
electric outlet die Steckdose
elevator der Fahrstuhl
e-mail *v* eine E-Mail senden;
  ~ *n* die E-Mail; **~ address** die
  E-Mail-Adresse
emergency der Notfall;
  ~ exit der Notausgang
empty *v* entleeren
end *v* beenden; **~** *n* das Ende
engaged (person) verlobt
English *adj* englisch; **~** *n*
  (language) das Englisch
engrave eingravieren
enjoy genießen
enter *v* **(place)** eintreten
entertainment die Unterhaltung
entrance der Eingang
envelope der Umschlag
epileptic *adj* epileptisch;
  ~ *n* der Epileptiker
equipment die Ausrüstung
escalator die Rolltreppe
e-ticket das E-Ticket
EU resident der EU-Bürger
euro der Euro
evening *n* der Abend

excess baggage das Übergepäck
exchange *v* umtauschen;
~ *n* (**place**) die Wechselstube; ~
rate der Wechselkurs
excursion der Ausflug
excuse *v* entschuldigen
exhausted erschöpft
exit *v* verlassen; ~ *n* der Ausgang
expensive teuer
experienced erfahren
expert der Experte
exposure (**film**) die Belichtung
express *adj* Express-; ~ **bus**
der Expressbus; ~ **train** der
Expresszug
extension (**phone**) die Durchwahl
extra *adj* zusätzlich; ~ **large**
extragroß
extract *v* (**tooth**) ziehen
eye das Auge
eyebrow wax
die Augenbrauenkorrektur

F

face *n* das Gesicht
facial *n* die kosmetische
Gesichtsbehandlung
family *n* die Familie
fan *n* (**appliance**) der Ventilator
far (**distance**) weit
farm der Bauernhof

far-sighted weitsichtig
fast *adj* schnell
fat free fettfrei
father der Vater
fax *v* faxen; ~ *n* das Fax;
~ **number** die Faxnummer
fee *n* die Gebühr
feed *v* füttern
ferry *n* die Fähre
fever *n* das Fieber
field (**sports**) der Platz
fill *v* (**car**) tanken
fill out *v* (**form**) ausfüllen
filling *n* (**tooth**) die Füllung
film *n* (**camera**) der Film
fine *n* (**fee for breaking law**)
die Strafe
finger *n* der Finger; ~**nail** der
Fingernagel
fire *n* das Feuer;
~ **department** die Feuerwehr; ~
door die Feuertür
first *adj* erste; ~ **class** erste Klasse
fit *n* (**clothing**) die Passform
fitting room die Umkleidekabine
fix *v* (**repair**) reparieren
fixed-price menu das Festpreismenü
flash photography das
Fotografieren mit Blitzlicht
flashlight das Blitzlicht
flight *n* der Flug

flip-flops die Badelatschen
floor *n* (**level**) die Etage
florist der Florist
flower *n* die Blume
folk music die Volksmusik
food das Essen; ~ **processor**
  die Küchenmaschine
foot *n* der Fuß
football game [BE] das Fußballspiel
for für
forecast *n* die Vorhersage
forest *n* der Wald
fork *n* die Gabel
form *n* (**document**) das Formular
formula (**baby**) die Babynahrung
fort die Festung
fountain *n* der Springbrunnen
free *adj* frei
freelance work die freiberufliche
  Arbeit
freezer der Gefrierschrank
fresh frisch
friend der Freund
frozen food die Tiefkühlkost
frying pan die Bratpfanne
full-time *adj* Vollzeit-

G

game *n* das Spiel
garage *n* (**parking**) die Garage; ~
  n (**for repairs**) die Autowerkstatt

garbage bag der Abfallbeutel
gas (**car**) das Benzin;
  ~ **station** die Tankstelle
gate (**airport**) das Gate
gay *adj* (**homosexual**) schwul;
  ~ **bar** die Schwulenbar;
  ~ **club** der Schwulenclub
gel *n* (**hair**) das Gel
generic drug das Generikum
German *adj* deutsch; ~ *n*
  (**language**) das Deutsch
Germany Deutschland
get off (**a train/bus/**
  subway) aussteigen
gift *n* das Geschenk; ~ **shop**
  der Geschenkwarenladen
girl das Mädchen; ~**friend**
  die Freundin
give *v* geben
glass (**drinking**) das Glas;
  ~ (**material**) das Glas
glasses die Brille
go *v* (**somewhere**) gehen
gold *n* das Gold
golf *n* das Golf; ~ **course**
  der Golfplatz; ~ **tournament**
  das Golfturnier
good *adj* gut; ~ *n* die Ware;
  ~ **afternoon** guten Tag
  ~ **day** guten Tag; ~ **evening**
  guten Abend; ~ **morning** guten

Morgen; **~bye** auf Wiedersehen

gram das Gramm

grandchild das Enkelkind

grandparents die Großeltern

gray *adj* grau

green *adj* grün

grocery store das Lebensmittelgeschäft

ground floor das Erdgeschoss

groundcloth die Unterlegplane

group *n* die Gruppe

guide *n* (**book**) der Reiseführer; ~ *n* (**person**) der Fremdenführer ~ **dog** der Blindenhund

gym *n* (**place**) der Fitnessraum

gynecologist der Gynäkologe

H

hair das Haar; **~brush** die Haarbürste; **~cut** der Haarschnitt; **~ dryer** der Fön; **~ salon** der Friseursalon; **~spray** das Haarspray; **~style** die Frisur; **~ stylist** der Friseur

halal halal

half *adj* halb; **~** *n* die Hälfte; **~ hour** die halbe Stunde; **~-kilo** das halbe Kilo

hammer *n* der Hammer

hand *n* die Hand; **~ luggage** das Handgepäck; **~ wash** die Handwäsche; **~bag [BE]** die Handtasche

handicapped behindert; **~-accessible** behindertengerecht

hangover der Kater

happy glücklich

hat der Hut

have *v* haben; **~ sex** Sex haben

hay fever der Heuschnupfen

head (body part) *n* der Kopf; **~ache** die Kopfschmerzen; **~phones** die Kopfhörer

health die Gesundheit; **~ food store** das Reformhaus

hearing impaired hörgeschädigt

heart das Herz; **~ condition** die Herzkrankheit

heat *v* heizen; **~er** das Heizgerät; **~ing [BE]** die Heizung

hectare der Hektar

hello Hallo

helmet der Helm

help *v* helfen; **~** *n* die Hilfe

here hier

hi Hallo

high hoch; **~chair** der Kindersitz; **~lights (hair)** die Strähnchen; **~way** die Autobahn

hiking boots die Wanderschuhe

hill n der Berg
hire v **[BE] (a car)** mieten;
  ~ car [BE] das Mietauto
hockey das Hockey
holiday [BE] der Urlaub
horsetrack die Pferderennbahn
hospital das Krankenhaus
hostel die Jugendherberge
hot (spicy) scharf;
  ~ (temperature) heiß;
  ~ spring heiße Quelle;
  ~ water heißes Wasser
hotel das Hotel
hour die Stunde
house n das Haus; **~hold
  goods** die Haushaltswaren;
  ~keeping services der
  Hotelservice
how wie; **~ much** wie viel
hug v umarmen
hungry hungrig
hurt v wehtun
husband der Ehemann

I

ibuprofen das Ibuprofen
ice n das Eis; **~ hockey** das
  Eishockey
icy eisig
identification die Identifikation
ill krank

in in
include v beinhalten
indoor pool (public) das Hallenbad
inexpensive preisgünstig
infected infiziert
information (phone) die Auskunft;
  ~ desk die Information
insect das Insekt: **~ bite** der
  Insektenstich; **~ repellent** der
  Insektenschutz
insert v **(card)** einführen
insomnia die Schlaflosigkeit
instant message die instant
  Message
insulin das Insulin
insurance die Versicherung;
  ~ card die Versicherungskarte;
  ~ company die
  Versicherungsgesellschaft
interesting interessant
intermediate fortgeschritten
international international;
  ~ flight der internationale Flug; **~
  student card** der internationale
  Studentenausweis
internet das Internet;
  ~ cafe das Internetcafé;
  ~ service der Internetservice
interpreter der Dolmetscher
intersection die Kreuzung
intestine der Darm

introduce *v* **(person)** vorstellen
invoice *n* [BE] die Rechnung
Ireland das Irland
Irish *adj* irisch
iron *v* bügeln; ~ *n* **(clothes)** das Bügeleisen
Italian *adj* italienisch

J

jacket *n* die Jacke
Japanese *adj* japanisch
jar *n* **(for jam etc.)** das Glas
jaw *n* der Kiefer
jazz *n* der Jazz; ~ **club** der Jazzclub
jeans die Jeans
jet ski *n* die Jet-Ski
jeweler der Juwelier
jewelry der Schmuck
join *v* **(go with somebody)** mitkommen
joint *n* **(body part)** das Gelenk

K

key *n* der Schlüssel; ~ **card** die Schlüsselkarte; ~**ring** der Schlüsselring
kiddie pool das Kinderbecken
kidney (body part) die Niere
kilo das Kilo; ~**gram** das Kilogramm; ~**meter** der Kilometer
kiss *v* küssen

kitchen die Küche; ~ **foil** [BE] die Aluminiumfolie
knee *n* das Knie
knife das Messer
kosher *adj* koscher

L

lace *n* **(fabric)** die Spitze
lactose intolerant laktoseintolerant
lake der See
large groß
last *adj* letzte
late (time) spät
launderette [BE] der Waschsalon
laundromat der Waschsalon
laundry (place) die Wäscherei ~ **service** der Wäscheservice
lawyer *n* der Anwalt
leather *n* das Leder
leave *v* **(hotel)** abreisen; ~ **(plane)** abfliegen
left *adj, adv* **(direction)** links
leg *n* das Bein
lens die Linse
less weniger
lesson *n* die Lektion; **take** ~**s** Unterricht nehmen
letter *n* der Brief
library die Bücherei
life jacket die Schwimmweste

lifeguard der Rettungsschwimmer
lift n [BE] der Fahrstuhl; ~ n
 (ride) die Mitfahrgelegenheit; ~
 pass der Liftpass
light n (cigarette) das Feuer;
 ~ n (overhead) die Lampe;
 ~bulb die Glühbirne
lighter n das Feuerzeug
like v mögen
line n (train/bus) die Linie
linen das Leinen
lip n die Lippe
liquor store das Spirituosengeschäft
liter der Liter
little wenig
live v leben; ~ music Livemusik
liver (body part) die Leber
loafers die Halbschuhe
local n (person) der Einheimische
lock v abschließen; ~ n das Schloss
locker das Schließfach
log off v (computer) abmelden
log on v (computer) anmelden
long adj lang; ~-sighted [BE]
 weitsichtig; ~-sleeved langärmlig
look v schauen; ~ for something
 etwas suchen
loose (fit) locker
lose v (something) verlieren
lost verloren; ~-and-found das
 Fundbüro

lotion die Lotion
louder lauter
love v (someone) lieben;
 ~ n die Liebe
low adj niedrig
luggage das Gepäck; ~ cart
 der Gepäckwagen; ~ locker das
 Gepäckschließfach;
 ~ ticket der Gepäckschein
lunch n das Mittagessen
lung die Lunge
luxury car das Luxusauto

M

machine washable
 maschinenwaschbar
magazine das Magazin
magnificent großartig
mail v mit der Post schicken; ~
 n die Post; ~box der Briefkasten
main attraction die Hauptattraktion
main course das Hauptgericht
mall das Einkaufszentrum
man (adult male) der Mann
manager der Manager
manicure n die Maniküre
manual car das Auto mit
 Gangschaltung
map n die Karte;
 ~ n (town) der Stadtplan
market n der Markt

married verheiratet
marry heiraten
mass *n* **(church service)** die Messe
massage *n* die Massage
match *n* das Spiel
meal die Mahlzeit
measure *v* **(someone)** Maß nehmen
measuring cup der Messbecher
measuring spoon der Messlöffel
mechanic *n* der Mechaniker
medication (drugs) die
  Medikamente
medicine das Medikament
medium (steak) medium
meet *v* treffen
meeting *n* **(business)** das Meeting;
  ~ room das Konferenzzimmer
membership card der
  Mitgliedsausweis
memorial (place) das Denkmal
memory card die Speicherkarte
mend *v* **(clothes)** ausbessern
menstrual cramps die
  Menstruationskrämpfe
menu (restaurant) die Speisekarte
message die Nachricht
meter *n* **(parking)** die Parkuhr; **~** *n*
  (measure) der Meter
microwave *n* die Mikrowelle
midday [BE] der Mittag
midnight die Mitternacht

mileage die Meilenzahl
mini-bar die Mini-Bar
minute die Minute
missing (not there) weg
mistake *n* der Fehler
mobile home der Wohnwagen
mobile phone [BE] das Handy
mobility die Mobilität
monastery das Kloster
money das Geld
month der Monat
mop *n* der Wischmopp
moped das Moped
more mehr
morning *n* der Morgen
mosque die Moschee
mother *n* die Mutter
motion sickness die Reisekrankheit
motor *n* der Motor;
  ~ boat das Motorboot;
  ~cycle das Motorrad;
  ~way [BE] die Autobahn
mountain der Berg;
  ~ bike das Mountainbike
mousse (hair) der Schaumfestiger
mouth *n* der Mund
movie der Film; **~ theater**
  das Kino
mug *v* überfallen
multiple-trip ticket
  der Mehrfachfahrschein

muscle n der Muskel
museum das Museum
music die Musik; ~ **store**
  das Musikgeschäft

N

nail file die Nagelfeile
nail salon das Nagelstudio
name n der Name
napkin die Serviette
nappy [BE] die Windel
nationality die Nationalität
nature preserve das Naturreservat
nausea die Übelkeit
nauseous übel
near nahe; ~**-sighted** kurzsichtig
nearby in der Nähe von
neck n der Nacken
necklace die Kette
need v brauchen
newspaper die Zeitung
newsstand der Zeitungskiosk
next adj nächste
nice schön
night die Nacht; ~**club** der
  Nachtclub
no nein; ~ **(not any)** kein
non-alcoholic nichtalkoholisch
non-smoking adj Nichtraucher
noon n der Mittag
north n der Norden

nose die Nase
note n **[BE] (money)** der Geldschein
nothing nichts
notify v benachrichtigen
novice der Anfänger
now jetzt
number n die Nummer
nurse n die Krankenschwester

O

office das Büro; ~ **hours**
  die Bürozeiten
off-licence [BE] das
  Spirituosengeschäft
oil n das Öl
OK okay
old adj alt
on the corner an der Ecke
once (one time) einmal
one ein; **(counting)** eins;
  ~**-day (ticket)** Tages-;
  ~**-way ticket (airline)** das
  einfache Ticket, **(bus/train/
  subway)** die Einzelfahrkarte;
  ~**-way street** die Einbahnstraße
only nur
open v öffnen; ~ adj offen
opera die Oper;
  ~ **house** das Opernhaus
opposite n das Gegenteil
optician der Optiker

orange *adj* **(color)** orange
orchestra das Orchester
order *v* **(restaurant)** bestellen
outdoor pool das Freibad
outside *prep* draußen
over *prep* **(direction)** über; **~done**
  (meat) zu lang
  gebraten; **~heat** *v* **(car)**
  überhitzen; **~look** *n* **(scenic**
  place) der Aussichtsplatz; **~night**
  über Nacht; **~-the-counter**
  (medication) rezeptfrei
oxygen treatment
  die Sauerstoffbehandlung

P

p.m. nachmittags
pacifier der Schnuller
pack *v* packen
package *n* das Paket
pad *n* **[BE]** die Monatsbinde
paddling pool [BE]
  das Kinderbecken
pain der Schmerz
pajamas der Pyjama
palace der Palast
pants die Hose
pantyhose die Strumpfhose
paper *n* **(material)** das Papier; **~**
  towel das Papierhandtuch
paracetamol [BE] das Paracetamol

park *v* parken; **~** *n* der Park; **~ing**
  garage das Parkhaus;
  ~ing lot der Parkplatz;
  ~ing meter die Parkuhr
parliament building
  das Parlamentsgebäude
part (for car) das Teil;
  ~-time *adj* Teilzeit-
pass through *v* **(travel)**
  durchreisen
passenger der Passagier
passport der Reisepass;
  ~ control die Passkontrolle
password das Passwort
pastry shop die Konditorei
patch *v* **(clothing)** ausbessern
path der Pfad
pay *v* bezahlen; **~phone**
  das öffentliche Telefon
peak *n* **(of a mountain)** der Gipfel
pearl *n* die Perle
pedestrian *n* der Fußgänger
pediatrician der Kinderarzt
pedicure *n* die Pediküre
pen *n* der Stift
penicillin das Penicillin
penis der Penis
per pro; **~ day** pro Tag;
  ~ hour pro Stunde;
  ~ night pro Nacht;
  ~ week pro Woche

perfume *n* das Parfüm

period (menstrual) die Periode; ~ **(of time)** der Zeitraum

permit *v* erlauben

petrol [BE] das Benzin; ~ **station [BE]** die Tankstelle

pewter das Zinn

pharmacy die Apotheke

phone *v* anrufen; ~ *n* das Telefon; ~ **call** das Telefonat; ~ **card** die Telefonkarte; ~ **number** die Telefonnummer

photo das Foto; ~**copy** die Fotokopie; ~**graphy** die Fotografie

pick up *v* **(person)** abholen

picnic area der Rastplatz

piece *n* das Stück

Pill (birth control) die Pille

pillow *n* das Kissen

pink *adj* rosa

piste [BE] die Piste; ~ **map [BE]** der Pistenplan

pizzeria die Pizzeria

place *v* **(a bet)** abgeben

plane *n* das Flugzeug

plastic wrap die Klarsichtfolie

plate *n* der Teller

platform [BE] (train) der Bahnsteig

platinum *n* das Platin

play *v* spielen; ~ *n* **(theatre)** das Stück; ~**ground** der Spielplatz;

~**pen** der Laufstall

please *adv* bitte

pleasure *n* die Freude

plunger die Saugglocke

plus size die Übergröße

pocket *n* die Tasche

poison *n* das Gift

poles (skiing) die Stöcke

police die Polizei; ~ **report** der Polizeibericht; ~ **station** das Polizeirevier

pond *n* der Teich

pool *n* der Pool

pop music die Popmusik

portion *n* die Portion

post *n* **[BE]** die Post; ~ **office** die Post; ~**box [BE]** der Briefkasten; ~**card** die Postkarte

pot *n* der Topf

pottery die Töpferwaren

pound *n* **(weight)** das Pfund; ~ **(British sterling)** das Pfund

pregnant schwanger

prescribe (medication) verschreiben

prescription das Rezept

press *v* **(clothing)** bügeln

price *n* der Preis

print *v* drucken; ~ *n* der Ausdruck

problem das Problem

produce *n* das Erzeugnis;
  ~ store das Lebensmittelgeschäft
prohibit verbieten
pronounce aussprechen
Protestant der Protestant
public *adj* öffentlich
pull *v* ziehen
purple *adj* violett
purse *n* die Handtasche
push *v* drücken; **~chair [BE]**
  der Kinderwagen

Q

quality *n* die Qualität
question *n* die Frage
quiet *adj* leise

R

racetrack die Rennbahn
racket *n* **(sports)** der Schläger
railway station [BE] der Bahnhof
rain *n* der Regen; **~coat** die
  Regenjacke; **~forest** der
  Regenwald; **~y** regnerisch
rap *n* **(music)** der Rap
rape *v* vergewaltigen;
  ~ *n* die Vergewaltigung
rare selten
rash *n* der Ausschlag
ravine die Schlucht
razor blade die Rasierklinge

reach *v* erreichen
ready bereit
real *adj* echt
receipt *n* die Quittung
receive *v* erhalten
reception (hotel) die Rezeption
recharge *v* aufladen
recommend empfehlen
recommendation die Empfehlung
recycling das Recycling
red *adj* rot
refrigerator der Kühlschrank
region die Region
registered mail das Einschreiben
regular *n* **(fuel)** das Normalbenzin
relationship die Beziehung
rent *v* mieten; **~** *n* die Miete
rental car das Mietauto
repair *v* reparieren
repeat *v* wiederholen
reservation die Reservierung;
  ~ desk der Reservierungsschalter
reserve *v* **(hotel)** reservieren
restaurant das Restaurant
restroom die Toilette
retired *adj* **(from work)** in Rente
return *v* **(something)**
  zurückgeben; **~** *n* **[BE] (trip)**
  die Hin- und Rückfahrt
reverse *v* **(the charges) [BE]**
  ein R-Gespräch führen

rib *n* **(body part)** die Rippe
right *adj, adv* **(direction)** rechts; ~
  of way die Vorfahrt
ring *n* der Ring
river der Fluss
road map die Straßenkarte
rob *v* berauben
robbed beraubt
romantic *adj* romantisch
room *n* das Zimmer; ~ **key**
  der Zimmerschlüssel;
  ~ **service** der Zimmerservice
round trip die Hin- und Rückfahrt
route *n* die Route
rowboat das Ruderboot
rubbing alcohol der
  Franzbranntwein
rubbish *n* [BE] der Abfall;
  ~ **bag** [BE] der Abfallbeutel
rugby das Rugby
ruin *n* die Ruine
rush *n* die Eile

S

sad traurig
safe *adj* **(protected)** sicher;
  ~ *n* **(thing)** der Safe
sales tax die Mehrwertsteuer
same *adj* gleiche
sandals die Sandalen
sanitary napkin die Monatsbinde

sauna die Sauna
sauté *v* sautieren
save *v* **(computer)** speichern
savings (account) das Sparkonto
scanner der Scanner
scarf der Schal
schedule *v* planen; ~ *n* der Plan
school *n* die Schule
science die Wissenschaft
scissors die Schere
sea das Meer
seat *n* der Sitzplatz
security die Sicherheit
see *v* sehen
self-service *n* die Selbstbedienung
sell *v* verkaufen
seminar das Seminar
send *v* senden
senior citizen der Rentner
separated (person) getrennt lebend
serious ernst
service (in a restaurant)
  die Bedienung
sexually transmitted disease
  (STD) die sexuell übertragbare
  Krankheit
shampoo *n* das Shampoo
sharp *adj* scharf
shaving cream die Rasiercreme
sheet *n* **(bed)** die Bettwäsche
ship *v* versenden

shirt das Hemd
shoe store das Schuhgeschäft
shoe der Schuh
shop v einkaufen;
~ n das Geschäft
shopping n das Einkaufen;
~ **area** das Einkaufszentrum;
~ **centre [BE]** das
Einkaufszentrum;
~ **mall** das Einkaufszentrum
short kurz; ~**-sleeved** kurzärmelig
shorts die kurze Hose
short-sighted [BE] kurzsichtig
shoulder n die Schulter
show v zeigen
shower n **(bath)** die Dusche
shrine der Schrein
sick adj krank
side n die Seite; ~ **dish** die Beilage;
~ **effect** die Nebenwirkung; ~
order die Beilage
sightseeing das Besichtigen von
Sehenswürdigkeiten;
~ **tour** die Besichtigungstour
sign v **(document)** unterschreiben
silk die Seide
silver n das Silber
single adj **(person)** alleinstehend;
~ **bed** das Einzelbett;
~ **print** der Einzelabzug;
~ **room** das Einzelzimmer

sink n das Waschbecken
sister die Schwester
sit v sitzen
size n die Größe
ski v Ski fahren; ~ n der Ski;
~ **lift** der Skilift
skin n die Haut
skirt n der Rock
sleep v schlafen; ~**er car**
der Schlafwagen; ~**ing bag**
der Schlafsack; ~**ing car [BE]** der
Schlafwagen
slice n die Scheibe
slippers die Pantoffeln
slower langsamer
slowly langsam
small klein
smoke v rauchen
smoking (area) Raucher-
snack bar der Imbiss
sneakers die Turnschuhe
snorkeling equipment
die Schnorchelausrüstung
snowboard n das Snowboard
snowshoe n der Schneeschuh
snowy verschneit
soap n die Seife
soccer der Fußball
sock die Socke
some (with singular nouns) etwas;
~ **(with plural nouns)** einige

soother [BE] der Schnuller
sore throat die Halsschmerzen
south n der Süden
souvenir n das Souvenir;
  ~ store das Souvenirgeschäft
spa das Wellness-Center
spatula der Spatel
speak v sprechen
specialist (doctor) der Spezialist
specimen die Probe
speeding die
  Geschwindigkeitsüberschreitung
spell v buchstabieren
spicy scharf; **~ (not bland)** würzig
spine (body part) die Wirbelsäule
spoon n der Löffel
sporting goods store
  das Sportgeschäft
sports der Sport; **~ massage**
  die Sportmassage
sprain n die Verstauchung
stadium das Stadion
stairs die Treppe
stamp v **(ticket)** entwerten;
  ~ n **(postage)** die Briefmarke
start v beginnen
starter [BE] die Vorspeise
station n **(stop)** die Haltestelle;
  bus ~ der Busbahnhof;
  gas ~ die Tankstelle;
  petrol ~ [BE] die Tankstelle;

subway ~ die U-Bahn-Haltestelle;
  train ~ der Bahnhof
statue die Statue
steakhouse das Steakhouse
steal v stehlen
steep adj steil
sterling silver das Sterlingsilber
sting n der Stich
stolen gestohlen
stomach der Magen; **~ache** die
  Bauchschmerzen
stool (bowel movement) der
  Stuhlgang
stop v **(bus)** anhalten;
  ~ n **(transportation)** die
  Haltestelle
store directory (mall)
  der Übersichtsplan
storey [BE] die Etage
stove n der Herd
straight adv **(direction)** geradeaus
strange seltsam
stream n der Strom
stroller (baby) der Kinderwagen
student (university) der Student;
  ~ (school) der Schüler
study v studieren;
  ~ing n das Studieren
stuffed gefüllt
stunning umwerfend
subtitle n der Untertitel

subway   die U-Bahn; ~ **station** die U-Bahn Haltestelle

suit *n* der Anzug; ~**case** der Koffer

sun *n* die Sonne; ~**block** das Sonnenschutzmittel; ~**burn** der Sonnenbrand; ~**glasses** die Sonnenbrille; ~**ny** sonnig; ~**screen** die Sonnencreme; ~**stroke** der Sonnenstich

super *n* (**fuel**) das Superbenzin; ~**market** der Supermarkt

surfboard das Surfboard

surgical spirit [BE] der Franzbranntwein

swallow *v* schlucken

sweater der Pullover

sweatshirt das Sweatshirt

sweet *n* [BE] die Süßigkeit; ~ *adj* (**taste**) süß

swelling die Schwellung

swim *v* schwimmen; ~**suit** der Badeanzug

symbol (**keyboard**) das Zeichen

synagogue die Synagoge

T

table *n* der Tisch

tablet (**medicine**) die Tablette

take *v* nehmen

tampon *n* der Tampon

taste *v* (**test**) kosten

taxi *n* das Taxi

team *n* das Team

teaspoon der Teelöffel

telephone *n* das Telefon

temple (**religious**) der Tempel

temporary vorübergehend

tennis das Tennis

tent *n* das Zelt; ~ **peg** der Zelthering; ~ **pole** die Zeltstange

terminal *n* (**airport**) der Terminal

terrible schrecklich

text *v* (**send a message**) eine SMS schicken; ~ *n* der Text

thank *v* danken; ~ **you** vielen Dank

the der?, das (neuter), die/

theater das Theater

theft der Diebstahl

there dort

thief der Dieb

thigh der Oberschenkel

thirsty durstig

this dieser?, dieses (neuter), diese/

throat der Hals

thunderstorm das Gewitter

ticket *n* die Fahrkarte; ~ **office** der Fahrkartenschalter

tie *n* (**clothing**) die Krawatte

tight (**fit**) eng

tights [BE] die Strumpfhose

time die Zeit; **~table [BE]**
(**transportation**) der Fahrplan
tire n der Reifen
tired müde
tissue das Gewebe
tobacconist der Tabakhändler
today adv heute
toe n der Zeh
toenail der Zehnagel
toilet [BE] die Toilette;
~ paper das Toilettenpapier
tomorrow adv morgen
tongue n die Zunge
tonight heute Abend
to (direction) zu
tooth der Zahn
toothpaste die Zahnpasta
total n (**amount**) der Gesamtbetrag
tough adj (**food**) zäh
tour n die Tour
tourist der Tourist;
~ information office das
Touristeninformationsbüro
tow truck der Abschleppwagen
towel n das Handtuch
tower n der Turm
town die Stadt; **~ hall** das Rathaus;
~ map der Stadtplan; **~ square**
der Rathausplatz
toy das Spielzeug;
~ store der Spielzeugladen

track n (**train**) der Bahnsteig
traditional traditionell
traffic light die Ampel
trail n (**ski**) die Piste;
~ map der Pistenplan
trailer (car) der Anhänger
train n der Zug;
~ station der Bahnhof
transfer v (**change trains/
flights**) umsteigen;
~ (money) überweisen
translate übersetzen
trash n der Abfall
travel n das Reisen;
~ agency das Reisebüro;
~ sickness die Reisekrankheit;
~ers check [cheque BE] der
Reisescheck
tree der Baum
trim (hair) v nachschneiden
trip n die Reise
trolley [BE] (grocery store)
der Einkaufswagen; **~ [BE]**
(**luggage**) der Gepäckwagen
trousers [BE] die Hose
T-shirt das T-Shirt
tumble dry maschinentrocknen
turn off v (**device**) ausschalten
turn on v (**device**) anschalten
TV der Fernseher
tyre [BE] der Reifen

U

ugly hässlich

umbrella der Regenschirm

unattended unbeaufsichtigt

unbranded medication [BE]
das Generikum

unconscious (faint) bewusstlos

underdone halb gar

underground *n* **[BE]** die U-Bahn; ~
station [BE] die U-Bahn-Haltestelle

underpants [BE] der Slip

understand *v* verstehen

underwear die Unterwäsche

unemployed arbeitslos

United Kingdom (U.K.)
das Großbritannien

United States (U.S.)
die Vereinigten Staaten

university die Universität

unleaded (gas) bleifrei

upset stomach
die Magenverstimmung

urgent dringend

urine der Urin

use *v* benutzen

username der Benutzername

utensil das Haushaltsgerät

V

vacancy (room) das freie Zimmer

vacation der Urlaub

vaccination die Impfung

vacuum cleaner der Staubsauger

vagina die Vagina

vaginal infection die vaginale
Entzündung

valid gültig

valley das Tal

valuable *adj* wertvoll

value *n* der Wert

van der Kleintransporter

VAT [BE] die Mehrwertsteuer

vegan *n* der Veganer;
~ *adj* vegan

vegetarian *n* der Vegetarier;
~ *adj* vegetarisch

vehicle registration
die Fahrzeugregistrierung

viewpoint (scenic) [BE]
der Aussichtsplatz

village das Dorf

vineyard das Weingut

visa das Visum

visit *v* besuchen; ~**ing hours** die
Besuchszeiten

visually impaired sehbehindert

vitamin das Vitamin

V-neck der V-Ausschnitt

volleyball game das
Volleyballspiel

vomit *v* erbrechen;
~**ing** das Erbrechen

W

wait v warten;
~ n die Wartezeit

waiter der Kellner

waiting room der Warteraum

waitress die Kellnerin

wake v wecken;
~-**up call** der Weckruf

walk v spazieren gehen;
~ n der Spaziergang;
~**ing route** die Wanderroute

wall clock die Wanduhr

wallet die Geldbörse

war memorial
das Kriegsdenkmal

warm v **(something)** erwärmen;
~ adj **(temperature)** warm

washing machine die
Waschmaschine

watch v beobachten

water ski n der Wasserski

waterfall der Wasserfall

wax v **(hair)** mit Wachs entfernen
(Haare)

weather n das Wetter

week die Woche; ~**end** das
Wochenende

weekly wöchentlich

welcome adj willkommen; **you're**
~ gern geschehen

well-rested ausgeruht

west n der Westen

what was

wheelchair der Rollstuhl;
~ **ramp** die Rollstuhlrampe

when adv **(at what time)** wann

where wo

white adj weiß; ~ **gold** das
Weißgold

who (question) wer

widowed verwitwet

wife die Ehefrau

window das Fenster;
~ **case** das Schaufenster

windsurfer (board)
das Surfbrett

wine list die Weinkarte

wireless wireless; ~ **phone** das
schnurlose Telefon

with mit

withdraw v **(money)** abheben;
~**al (bank)** die Abhebung

without ohne

woman die Frau

wool die Wolle

work v arbeiten

wrap v einpacken

wrist das Handgelenk

write v schreiben

Y

year das Jahr

yellow *adj* gelb; **~ gold** *n* das
   Gelbgold
yes ja
yesterday *adv* gestern
young *adj* jung

youth hostel
   die Jugendherberge

Z

zoo der Zoo

German–English

A

der Abend evening
das Abendessen dinner
der Abfall *n* trash [rubbish BE]
der Abfallbeutel garbage [rubbish
   BE] bag
abfliegen *v* leave (plane)
der Abflug departure (plane)
abgeben *v* place (a bet)
abheben *v* withdraw (money)
die Abhebung withdrawal (bank)
abholen *v* pick up (something)
ablehnen *v* decline (credit card)
abmelden *v* log off (computer)
der Abschleppwagen tow truck
abschließen *v* lock (door)
der Adapter adapter
die Adresse *n* address
das Aftershave aftershave
die Agentur agency
AIDS AIDS
die Akupunktur *n* acupuncture

akzeptieren *v* accept
allein alone; **~stehend** single
   (person)
allergisch allergic;
die allergische Reaktion allergic
   reaction
alt *adj* old
das Alter *n* age
die Alternativroute alternate route
die Aluminiumfolie aluminum
   [kitchen BE] foil
amerikanisch American
die Ampel traffic light
anämisch anemic
die Anästhesie anesthesia
der Anfänger beginner/novice
angreifen *v* attack
anhalten *v* stop
der Anhänger trailer
ankommen arrive
die Ankunft arrival
anmelden *v* log on (computer)

der Anruf n call
anrufen v call
anschalten v turn on (device)
ansteckend contagious
das Antibiotikum n antibiotic
das Antiquitätengeschäft
  antiques store
antiseptisch antiseptic
der Anwalt lawyer
die Anzahlung n deposit (car rental)
der Anzug n suit
das Apartment apartment
die Apotheke pharmacy [chemist
  BE]
arbeiten v work
arbeitslos adj unemployed
der Arm n arm (body part)
die Aromatherapie aromatherapy
die Arterie artery
die Arthritis arthritis
der Arzt doctor
asiatisch Asian
das Aspirin aspirin
asthmatisch asthmatic
atmen breathe (place)
attraktiv attractive
auf Wiedersehen goodbye
aufladen v recharge
das Auge eye
ausbessern v mend (clothing)
der Ausfluss discharge (bodily fluid)

ausfüllen v fill out (form)
der Ausgang n exit
ausgeschlafen well-rested
die Auskunft information (phone)
die Ausrüstung equipment
ausschalten turn off (device)
der Ausschlag rash
der Aussichtsplatz viewpoint [BE]
aussprechen pronounce
aussteigen get off (a train/bus/
  subway)
Australien Australia
der Australier Australian
das Auto car; ~ **mit**
  Automatikschaltung
  automatic car; ~ **mit**
  Gangschaltung manual car
die Autobahn highway [motorway
  BE]
automatisch automatic
der Autositz car seat
die Autovermietung car rental
  [hire BE]

B

das Baby baby
die Babyflasche baby bottle
die Babynahrung formula (baby)
das Baby-Pflegetuch baby wipe
der Babysitter babysitter
backen bake

die Bäckerei bakery
das Bad bathroom
der Badeanzug swimsuit
die Badelatschen flip-flops
der Bahnhof train [railway BE] station
der Bahnsteig track [platform BE]
das Ballett ballet
die Bank bank (money)
der Bankautomat ATM
die Bankkarte ATM card
die Bar bar (place)
das Bargeld n cash
der Baseball baseball (game)
der Basketball basketball (game)
die Batterie battery
die Bauchschmerzen stomachache
der Bauernhof n farm
der Baum tree
die Baumwolle cotton
die Beaufsichtigung supervision
die Bedienung service (in a restaurant)
beenden v exit (computer)
beginnen begin
behindert handicapped;
~engerecht handicapped [disabled BE]-accessible
beige adj beige
die Beilage side order
das Bein leg

beinhalten include (tax)
die Bekleidung clothing
das Bekleidungsgeschäft clothing store
belasten v charge (credit card)
belästigen bother
die Belichtung exposure (film)
benachrichtigen notify
benutzen v use
der Benutzername username
das Benzin gas [petrol BE]
beobachten v watch
der Berater consultant
berauben rob
beraubt robbed
bereit ready
der Berg hill; ~ mountain
beschädigen v damage
beschädigt damaged
die Beschwerde complaint
die Beschwerden condition (medical)
der Besen broom
die Besichtigungstour sightseeing tour
besser better
bestätigen confirm
beste adj best
bestellen v order (restaurant)
besuchen v visit
die Besuchszeiten visiting hours

das Bett *n* bed
die Bettwäsche sheets
bewusstlos unconscious (condition)
bezahlen pay
die Beziehung relationship
der BH bra
der Bikini bikini
billig cheap
billiger cheaper
bitte please
die Blase bladder
blau *adj* blue
bleifrei unleaded (gas)
der Blinddarm appendix (body part)
der Blindenhund guide dog
das Blitzlicht flashlight
die Blume *n* flower
die Bluse blouse
das Blut blood
der Blutdruck blood pressure
bluten bleed
der Blutstau congestion
das Boot boat
die Bordkarte boarding pass
der botanische Garten botanical garden
der Boxkampf boxing match
die Bratpfanne frying pan
brauchen *v* need
braun *adj* brown
brechen *v* break

die Bremse brakes (car)
brennen *v* burn
der Brief letter
der Briefkasten mailbox [postbox BE]
die Briefmarke *n* stamp (postage)
die Brille glasses (optical)
bringen bring
britisch British
die Brosche brooch
die Brücke bridge
der Bruder brother
die Brust breast; ~ chest
~schmerzen chest pain
das Buch *n* book
die Bücherei library
der Buchladen bookstore
buchstabieren *v* spell
das Bügeleisen *n* iron (clothes)
bügeln *v* iron
das Büro office
die Bürozeiten office hours
der Bus bus; ~**bahnhof** bus station; ~**fahrschein** bus ticket
die Bushaltestelle bus stop;
die Business-Class business class
die Bustour bus tour

C

das Café cafe (place)
campen *v* camp

der Campingkocher camping stove
der Campingplatz campsite
die Campingtoilette chemical toilet
der Canyon canyon
das Casino casino
die CD CD
Celsius Celsius
das Check-in check-in
das Check-out check-out
chinesisch Chinese
der Club *n* club
der Computer computer
die Creme *n* cream (ointment)

D

danken thank
der Darm intestine
das (neuter) the
das Datum *n* date (calendar)
die Decke blanket
das Denkmal memorial (place)
das Deodorant deodorant
der the
das Deutsch German;
~**land** Germany
der Diabetiker *n* diabetic
der Diamant diamond
die the
der Dieb thief; ~**stahl** theft
diese this

der Diesel diesel
dieser this
dieses (neuter) this
digital digital
der Digitaldruck digital print
das Digitalfoto digital photo
die Digitalkamera digital camera
das Display *n* display
Dollar dollar (U.S.)
der Dolmetscher interpreter
das Doppelbett double bed
das Dorf village
dort there
der Dosenöffner can opener
draußen outside
dringend urgent
drucken *v* print
drücken *v* push
dunkel *adj* dark
der Durchfall diarrhea
durchreisen pass through
durstig thirsty
die Dusche *n* shower
das Dutzend dozen
die DVD DVD

E

echt real
die EC-Karte debit card
die Ecke *n* corner; **an der Ecke** on the corner

die Economy-Class economy class

die Ehefrau wife

der Ehemann husband

die Eile *n* rush

die Einbahnstraße one-way street

einbrechen *v* break in (burglary)

einchecken *v* check in

einführen *v* insert

der Eingang entrance

eingravieren engrave

der Einheimische *n* local (person)

einkaufen *v* shop

das Einkaufen shopping

der Einkaufskorb basket (grocery store)

der Einkaufswagen cart [trolley BE] (grocery store)

das Einkaufszentrum shopping mall [centre BE]; **~** shopping area (town)

einlösen *v* cash (check)

einmal once

einpacken *v* wrap (parcel)

eins one

das Einschreiben registered mail

einsteigen *v* board (bus)

eintreten *v* enter

der Eintritt admission (fee)

der Einwegartikel *n* disposable

der Einweg-Rasierer disposable razor

einzahlen *v* deposit (money)

die Einzahlung *n* deposit (bank)

der Einzelabzug single print

das Einzelbett single bed

das Einzelzimmer single room

das Eis *n* ice; **~hockey** ice hockey

der Ellenbogen elbow

die E-Mail *n* e-mail; **~-Adresse** e-mail address; **~ senden** *v* e-mail

empfehlen recommend

die Empfehlung recommendation

eng tight (fit)

englisch English

der Enkel grandchild

entleeren *v* empty

entschuldigen *v* excuse

entwerten *v* stamp (ticket)

entwickeln *v* develop (film)

epileptisch *adj* epileptic

erbrechen *v* vomit

erfahren *adj* experienced

erhalten receive

die Erkältung *n* cold (sickness)

erklären explain

erlauben allow

ernst serious

erreichen *v* reach

erschöpft exhausted

erstaunlich amazing

erste Klasse first class

erste *adj* first
erwärmen *v* warm (something)
essen eat
das Essen food
das Esszimmer dining room
die Etage floor [storey BE]
das E-Ticket e-ticket
etwas something;
  ~ mehr... some more...
der EU-Bürger EU resident
der Euro euro
die Exkursion excursion
der Experte *n* expert
der Express *n* express;
  ~bus express bus
extra extra; **~ groß** extra large

F

die Fähre ferry
fahren *v* drive
die Fahrkarte ticket
der Fahrkartenschalter ticket office
das Fahrrad *n* bicycle
der Fahrradweg bike route
der Fahrstuhl elevator [lift BE]
die Fahrzeugregistrierung vehicle registration
die Familie family
die Farbe *n* color
das Fax *n* fax
faxen *v* fax

die Faxnummer fax number
der Fehler *n* mistake
fehlen be missing
der Urlaub vacation [holiday BE]
das Feinkostgeschäft delicatessen
das Fenster window
der Fernseher television
das Festpreismenü fixed-price menu
die Festung fort
fettfrei fat free
das Feuer *n* fire
die Feuertür fire door
die Feuerwehr fire department
das Feuerzeug lighter
das Fieber fever
filetiert fileted (food)
der Film film (camera);
  ~ movie (cinema)
der Finger *n* finger
der Fingernagel fingernail
der Fitnessraum gym (workout)
die Flasche *n* bottle
der Flaschenöffner bottle opener
der Fleischer butcher
der Florist florist
der Flug flight
die Fluggesellschaft airline
der Flughafen airport
das Flugzeug airplane
der Fluss river

der Fön hair dryer
das Förderband conveyor belt
das Formular n form
fortgeschritten intermediate
das Foto photo
die Fotografie photography
fotografieren take a photo
die Fotokopie photocopy
die Frage n question
der Franzbranntwein rubbing alcohol [surgical spirit BE]
die Frau woman
freiberufliche Arbeit freelance work
frei adj free
das Fremdenverkehrsbüro tourist information office
die Freude pleasure
der Freund boyfriend; friend
die Freundin girlfriend; friend
frisch fresh
die Frischhaltefolie plastic wrap
der Friseur barber, hairstylist
der Friseursalon hair salon
die Frisur hairstyle
früh early
das Frühstück breakfast
der Führer guide
die Führerscheinnummer driver's license number
das Fundbüro lost-and-found

für for
der Fuß foot; ~**ball** soccer
das Fußballspiel soccer match [football game BE]
der Fußgänger n pedestrian
das Fußgelenk n ankle
füttern v feed

G

die Gabel fork
der Gang aisle
die Garage garage
das Gate gate (airport)
das Gebäude building
geben v give
die Gebühr fee
der Geburtstag birthday
gefährlich dangerous
der Gefrierschrank freezer
das Gegenteil n opposite
gehen v go (somewhere)
gekocht stewed
das Gel gel (hair)
gelb adj yellow
das Gelbgold yellow gold
das Geld money
die Geldbörse wallet
der Geldschein n bill [note BE] (money)
das Gelenk joint (body part)
das Generikum generic drug

[unbranded medication BE]
genießen *v* enjoy
das Gepäck baggage [luggage BE]
die Gepäckausgabe baggage claim
der Gepäckschein baggage
  [luggage BE] ticket
das Gepäckschließfach baggage
  [luggage BE] locker
der Gepäckwagen baggage
  [luggage BE] cart
geradeaus straight
gern geschehen you're welcome
das Geschäft business; ~ store
  ~**sverzeichnis** store directory;
  ~**szentrum** business center
das Geschenk gift
der Geschenkwarenladen
  gift shop
das Geschirr dishes (kitchen)
der Geschirrspüler dishwasher
das Geschirrspülmittel
  dishwashing liquid
geschlossen closed
die Geschwindigkeitsüber-
  schreitung speeding
das Gesicht *n* face
gestern yesterday
gestohlen stolen
die Gesundheit health
das Getränk *n* drink
die Getränkekarte drink menu

getrennt lebend separated
  (person)
das Gewitter thunderstorm
gewürfelt diced (food)
das Gift *n* poison
der Gipfel peak (of a mountain)
das Girokonto checking [current
  BE] account
das Glas glass
gleich same
glücklich happy
die Glühbirne lightbulb
golden golden
der Golfplatz golf course
das Golfturnier golf
  tournament
das Grad degree (temperature)
das Gramm gram
grau *adj* gray
der Grill *n* barbecue
groß big; ~ large
großartig magnificent
das Großbritannien United
  Kingdom (U.K.)
die Größe *n* size
die Großeltern grandparents
größer bigger; ~ larger
grün *adj* green
die Gruppe *n* group
gültig valid
der Gürtel belt

gut *adj* good; *adv* well;
  ~en Abend good evening;
  ~en Morgen good morning;
  ~en Tag good day
der Gynäkologe gynecologist

H

das Haar hair
die Haarbürste hairbrush
der Harfestiger mousse (hair)
der Haarschnitt haircut
das Haarspray hairspray
haben *v* have
halal halal
halb half; **~gar** underdone;
  die ~e Stunde half hour;
  das ~e Kilo half-kilo
die Halbschuhe loafers
halbtags part-time
das Hallenbad indoor pool
Hallo hello
der Hals throat
die Halsschmerzen sore throat
die Haltestelle *n* stop
der Hammer *n* hammer
die Hand *n* hand
das Handgelenk wrist
das Handgepäck hand luggage
die Handtasche purse [handbag BE]
das Handtuch towel
Handwäsche hand wash

das Handy cell [mobile BE] phone
hässlich ugly
die Hauptattraktion main
  attraction
das Hauptgericht main course
das Haus *n* house
das Haushaltsgerät utensil
die Haushaltswaren household
  goods
die Haut *n* skin
heiraten *v* marry
heiß hot (temperature);
  ~e Quelle hot spring;
  ~es Wasser hot water
heizen *v* heat
die Heizung heating
der Hektar hectare
helfen *v* help
der Helm helmet
das Hemd shirt
der Herd stove
das Herz heart
die Herzkrankheit heart condition
der Heuschnupfen hay fever
heute today; **~ Abend** tonight
hier here
die Hilfe *n* help
die Hin- und Rückfahrt round-trip
Hinfahrt- one-way (ticket)
hinter behind (direction)
hoch high

das Hockey hockey
die Höhle n cave
hörgeschädigt hearing impaired
die Hose pants [trousers BE]
das Hotel hotel
hungrig hungry
husten v cough
der Husten n cough
der Hut hat

I

das Ibuprofen ibuprofen
die Identifikation identification
die Impfung vaccination
in in
infiziert infected
die Information information;
  ~ information desk
inländisch domestic
der Inlandsflug domestic flight
das Insekt bug
der Insektenschutz insect repellent
der Insektenstich insect bite
die Instant Message instant
  message
das Insulin insulin
interessant interesting
international international;
  der ~e Studentenausweis
  international student card;
  der ~e Flug international flight

das Internet internet;
  ~café internet cafe
der Internet-service internet service
irisch adj Irish
Irland Ireland
italienisch adj Italian

J

ja yes
die Jacke jacket
das Jahr year
japanisch Japanese
der Jazz jazz; **~club** jazz club
die Jeans jeans
der Jeansstoff denim
der Jet-ski jet ski
jetzt now
die Jugendherberge hostel;
  ~ youth hostel
jung adj young
der Junge boy
der Juwelier jeweler

K

das Kabarett cabaret
das Kaffeehaus coffee house
die Kalorie calorie
kalt adj cold (temperature);
  ~ cool (temperature)
die Kamera camera
die Kameratasche camera case

der Kamm n comb
das Kanada Canada
kanadisch adj Canadian
die Karaffe carafe
die Karte n card; ~ map
der Kassierer cashier
der Kater hangover (alcohol)
die Kathedrale cathedral
kaufen v buy
das Kaufhaus department store
der Kaugummi chewing gum
der Kellner waiter
die Kellnerin waitress
die Kette necklace
der Kiefer jaw
das Kilo kilo;
   ~gramm kilogram
der Kilometer kilometer
das Kind child
der Kinderarzt pediatrician
das Kinderbecken kiddie pool
das Kinderbett cot
die Kinderkarte children's menu
die Kinderportion children's
   portion
der Kindersitz highchair
der Kinderstuhl child's seat;
der Kinderwagen stroller
das Kino movie theater
die Kirche church
das Kissen pillow

die Klarsichtfolie plastic wrap
   [cling film BE]
die Klasse class
die klassische Musik classical music
das Kleid n dress (clothing)
die Kleiderordnung dress code
klein small
der Kleintransporter van
die Klimaanlage air conditioning
die Klippe cliff
das Kloster monastery
das Knie n knee
der Knochen n bone
kochen v boil; ~ cook
das Kölnischwasser cologne
der Koffer suitcase
der Kollege colleague
kommen v come
die Konditorei pastry shop
das Kondom condom
die Konferenz conference
das Konferenzzimmer meeting
   room
der Kongressaal convention hall
die Konserve canned good
das Konsulat consulate
kontaktieren v contact
die Kontaktlinse contact lens
die Kontaktlinsenlösung contact
   lens solution
das Konto n account

das Konzert concert
die Konzerthalle concert hall
der Kopf *n* head (body part)
die Kopfhörer headphones
die Kopfschmerzen headache
der Korkenzieher corkscrew
koscher kosher
kosmetisch *adj* cosmetic;
   ~e Gesichtsbehandlung
   facial (treatment)
kosten *v* cost; **~** taste
krank ill; **~** sick
das Krankenhaus hospital
die Krankenschwester *n* nurse
der Krankenwagen ambulance
die Krawatte tie (clothing)
die Kreditkarte credit card
die Kreuzung intersection
das Kriegsdenkmal war
   memorial
das Kristall crystal (glass)
die Küche kitchen
die Küchenmaschine food
   processor
der Kühlschrank refrigerator
die Kunst art
das Kupfer copper
kurz short; **~e Hose** shorts
kurzärmelig short-sleeved
kurzsichtig near- [short- BE] sighted
küssen *v* kiss

L

laktoseintolerant lactose
   intolerant
die Lampe *n* light (overhead)
die Landesvorwahl country code
landwirtschaftliches
   Erzeugnis produce
lang *adj* long; **~ärmlig** long-
   sleeved;
langsam slow;
   ~er slower
langweilig boring
der Laufstall playpen
lauter louder
leben *v* live
das Lebensmittelgeschäft
   grocery store
die Leber liver (body part)
lecker delicious
das Leder leather
leicht easy
das Leinen linen
leise quiet
die Lektion lesson
letzte *adj* last
die Liebe *n* love
lieben *v* love (someone)
der Liegestuhl deck chair (ferry)
der Liftpass lift pass
die Linie line (train)
links left (direction)

die Linse lens
die Lippe lip
der Liter liter
Livemusik live music
locker loose (fit)
der Löffel *n* spoon
löschen *v* clear (on an ATM);
~ *v* delete (computer)
die Lotion lotion
die Luftpost *n* airmail
die Luftpumpe air pump
lufttrocknen *v* air dry
die Lunge lung

M

das Mädchen girl
das Magazin magazine
der Magen stomach
die Magenverstimmung upset
stomach
die Mahlzeit meal
der Manager manager
die Maniküre *n* manicure
der Mann man (male)
der Mantel *n* coat
der Markt market
maschinentrocknen tumble dry
die Massage *n* massage
mechanisch *adj* mechanic
das Medikament medicine
die Medikamente medication

medium *adj* medium (meat)
das Meer sea
mehr more
die Mehrwertsteuer sales tax
[VAT BE]
die Menstruationskrämpfe
menstrual cramps
die Messe mass (church service)
messen *v* measure (someone)
das Messer knife
der Messbecher measuring cup
der Messlöffel measuring spoon
das Mietauto rental [hire BE] car
mieten *v* rent [hire BE]
die Mikrowelle *n* microwave
mild mild
die Mini-Bar mini-bar
die Minute minute
mit with; ~ **Bedienung** full-service
die Mitgliedskarte membership
card
mitkommen *v* join
mitnehmen give somebody a lift
(ride)
Mittag noon [midday BE]
das Mittagessen *n* lunch
Mitternacht midnight
der Mixer blender
die Mobilität mobility
mögen *v* like
der Monat month

die Monatsbinde sanitary napkin
[pad BE]
der Mopp *n* mop
das Moped moped
morgen tomorrow
der Morgen morning
die Moschee mosque
der Moslem Muslim
das Motorboot motor boat
das Motorrad motorcycle
das Mountainbike mountain bike
müde tired
der Mund mouth
die Münze coin
das Münztelefon pay phone
das Museum museum
die Musik music
das Musikgeschäft music store
der Muskel muscle
die Mutter mother

N

nach after
der Nachmittag afternoon
nachprüfen *v* check (on something)
die Nachricht message
nachschneiden trim (haircut)
nächste *adj* next
die Nacht night
der Nachtclub nightclub
der Nacken neck

die Nagelfeile nail file
das Nagelstudio nail salon
nahe *prep* near
die Nähe vicinity;
in der Nähe nearby
der Name *n* name
die Nase nose
die Nationalität nationality
das Naturreservat nature preserve
die Nebenstelle extension (phone)
die Nebenwirkung side effect
nehmen *v* take
nein no
Nichtraucher- non-smoking (area)
nichts nothing
niedrig low
die Niere kidney (body part)
der Norden *n* north
normal regular
der Notausgang emergency exit
der Notfall emergency
die Nummer *n* number
nur only; ~ just

O

obere *adj* upper
der Oberschenkel thigh
offen *adj* open
öffentlich *adj* public
öffnen *v* open
die Öffnungszeiten business hours

ohne without
das Ohr ear
die Ohrenschmerzen earache
der Ohrring earring
OK okay
das Öl *n* oil
die Oper opera
das Opernhaus opera house
der Optiker optician
orange *adj* orange (color)
das Orchester orchestra
die Ortsvorwahl area code
der Osten *n* east

P

packen *v* pack
die Packung carton;
~ packet
das Paket package
der Palast palace
paniert breaded
die Panne breakdown (car)
die Pantoffeln slippers
das Papier *n* paper
das Papierhandtuch paper towel
das Paracetamol acetaminophen
[paracetamol BE]
das Parfüm *n* perfume
der Park *n* park
parken *v* park
das Parkhaus parking garage

der Parkplatz parking lot [car
park BE]
die Parkuhr parking meter
das Parlamentsgebäude
parliament building
das Parterre ground floor
der Passagier passenger
die Passform fit (clothing)
die Passkontrolle passport
control
das Passwort password
die Pediküre pedicure
das Penicillin penicillin
der Penis penis
die Pension bed and breakfast
die Periode period (menstrual)
die Perle pearl
der Pfad path
die Pferderennbahn horsetrack
das Pflaster bandage
das Pfund *n* pound (weight)
das Pfund pound (British sterling)
die Pille Pill (birth control)
die Piste *n* trail [piste BE]
der Pistenplan trail [piste BE] map
die Pizzeria pizzeria
der Plan *n* schedule [timetable BE];
~ map
planen *v* plan
das Platin platinum
der Platte flat tire

der Platz field (sports); ~ seat; ~ **am Gang** aisle seat
die Plombe filling (tooth)
der Po buttocks
die Polizei police
der Polizeibericht police report
das Polizeirevier police station
der Pool n pool
die Popmusik pop music
die Portion n portion
die Post mail [post BE]; ~ post office
die Postkarte postcard
der Preis price; ~ **pro Gedeck** cover charge
preisgünstig inexpensive
pro per; ~ **Nacht** per night; ~ **Stunde** per hour; ~ **Tag** per day; ~ **Woche** per week
das Problem problem
Prost! Cheers!
die Prothese denture
die Puppe doll
der Pyjama pajamas

Q

die Qualität n quality
die Quittung receipt

R

das R-Gespräch collect call [reverse charge call BE]
ein R-Gespräch führen v call collect [to reverse the charges BE]
der Rabatt discount
das Radfahren cycling
der Rap rap (music)
die Rasiercreme shaving cream
die Rasierklinge razor blade
der Rastplatz picnic area
das Rathaus town hall
der Rathausplatz town square
rauchen v smoke
Raucher- smoking (area)
die Rechnung bill [invoice BE] (of sale)
rechts right (direction)
das Recycling recycling
das Reformhaus health food store
der Regen n rain
die Regenjacke raincoat
der Regenschirm umbrella
der Regenwald rainforest
die Region region
regnerisch rainy
der Reifen tire [tyre BE]
reinigen v clean; **chemisch** ~ dry clean
die Reinigung dry cleaner's
die Reinigungsmittel cleaning supplies
die Reise trip; ~ journey
das Reisebüro travel agency

der Reiseführer guide book
die Reisekrankheit motion sickness
der Reisepass passport
der Reisescheck traveler's check
  [cheque BE]
die Rennbahn racetrack
der Rentner senior citizen
reparieren *v* fix; ~ repair
reservieren *v* reserve
die Reservierung reservation
der Reservierungsschalter
  reservation desk
das Restaurant restaurant
der Rettungsschwimmer lifeguard
das Rezept prescription
die Rezeption reception
die Richtung direction
der Ring *n* ring
die Rippe rib (body part)
der Rock skirt
der Rollstuhl wheelchair
die Rollstuhlrampe wheelchair
  ramp
die Rolltreppe escalator
romantisch romantic
rosa *adj* pink
rot *adj* red
die Route route
der Rücken *n* back (body part)
die Rückenschmerzen backache
der Rucksack backpack

das Ruderboot rowboat
das Rugby rugby
die Ruine ruin

S

der Safe *n* safe (for valuables)
die Sandalen sandals
sauber *adj* clean
die Sauerstoffbehandlung
  oxygen treatment
die Saugglocke plunger
die Sauna sauna
der Scanner scanner
die Schachtel *n* pack; ~
  Zigaretten pack of cigarettes
der Schal scarf
scharf hot (spicy); ~ sharp
das Schaufenster window case
der Scheck *n* check [cheque BE]
  (payment)
die Schere scissors
schicken send;
  per Post ~ mail
das Schlachtfeld battleground
schlafen *v* sleep
die Schläfrigkeit drowsiness
der Schlafsack sleeping bag
die Schlafstörung insomnia
der Schlafwagen sleeper [sleeping
  BE] car
der Schläger racket (sports)

schlecht nauseous; ~ bad

der Schlepplift drag lift

schließen v close (a shop)

das Schließfach locker

das Schloss castle; ~ lock

die Schlucht ravine

der Schlüssel key; **~ring** key ring

die Schlüsselkarte key card

der Schmerz pain; **Schmerzen haben** be in pain

der Schmuck jewelry

schmutzig dirty

der Schneeschuh snowshoe

schneiden v cut

schnell fast

der Schnellzug express train

der Schnitt n cut (injury)

der Schnuller pacifier [soother BE]

schön nice; ~ beautiful

schrecklich terrible

schreiben write

der Schrein shrine

der Schuh shoe

das Schuhgeschäft shoe store

die Schule school

die Schulter shoulder

die Schüssel bowl

schwanger pregnant

schwarz adj black

die Schwellung swelling

die Schwester sister

schwierig difficult

das Schwimmbad swimming pool

schwimmen v swim

die Schwimmweste life jacket

schwindelig dizzy

schwul adj gay

die Schwulenbar gay bar

der Schwulenclub gay club

der See lake

sehbehindert visually impaired

sehen v look; ~ see

die Sehenswürdigkeit attraction

die Seide silk

die Seife n soap

die Seilbahn cable car

sein v be

die Selbstbedienung self-service

selten rare

seltsam strange

das Seminar seminar

senden v send

die Serviette napkin

der Sessellift chair lift

sexuell übertragbare Krankheit sexually transmitted disease (STD)

das Shampoo n shampoo

sich scheiden lassen v divorce

sicher adj safe (protected)

die Sicherheit security

das Sieb colander
das Sightseeing sightseeing
das Silber *n* silver
sitzen *v* sit
der Ski *n* ski
Ski fahren *v* ski
der Skilift ski lift
der Slip briefs (clothing)
die SMS SMS;
eine SMS schicken *v* text (message)
das Snowboard *n* snowboard
die Socke sock
die Sonne *n* sun
der Sonnenbrand sunburn
die Sonnenbrille sunglasses
die Sonnencreme sunscreen
der Sonnenstich sunstroke
sonnig sunny
das Souvenir souvenir; **~geschäft** souvenir store
das Sparkonto savings (account)
spät late (time)
der Spatel spatula
später later
spazieren gehen *v* walk
der Spaziergang *n* walk
die Speicherkarte memory card
speichern *v* save (computer)
die Speisekarte menu
der Spezialist specialist (doctor)
das Spiel game; **~** match

spielen *v* play
die Spielhalle arcade
der Spielplatz playground
das Spielzeug toy
der Spielzeugladen toy store
das Spirituosengeschäft liquor store [off-licence BE]
die Spitze lace (fabric)
der Sport sports
die Sportmassage sports massage
das Sportgeschäft sporting goods store
sprechen *v* speak
der Springbrunnen fountain
die Spülung conditioner (hair)
die Stäbchen chopsticks
das Stadion stadium
die Stadt city; **~** town
der Stadtplan town map
die Stadtrundfahrt sightseeing tour
das Stadtzentrum downtown area
die Stange carton (of cigarettes)
die Statue statue
der Staubsauger vacuum cleaner
das Steakhouse steakhouse
die Steckdose electric outlet
stehlen *v* steal
steil steep
das Sterlingsilber sterling silver
der Stich *n* sting

die Stiefel boots
der Stift pen
stillen breastfeed
die Stöcke poles (skiing)
stornieren *v* cancel
die Strafe *n* fine (fee for breaking law)
die Strähnchen highlights (hair)
der Strand beach
die Straßenkarte road map
der Strom electricity
die Strumpfhose pantyhose [tights BE]
das Stück *n* piece; ~ play (theater); ~ slice
der Student student
studieren *v* study
der Stuhl chair
der Stuhlgang stool (bowel movement)
die Stunde hour
der Süden *n* south
das Super super (fuel)
der Supermarkt supermarket
das Surfboard surfboard
das Surfbrett windsurfer (board)
süß cute; ~ sweet (taste)
die Süßigkeit candy [sweet BE]
das Sweatshirt sweatshirt
die Synagoge synagogue
synchronisiert dubbed

T

der Tabakhändler tobacconist
die Tablette tablet (medicine)
der Tag day
Tages- one-day (ticket)
das Tal valley
der Tampon tampon
tanken *v* fill (car)
die Tankstelle gas [petrol BE] station
der Tanzclub dance club
tanzen *v* dance
die Tasche bag; ~ pocket
die Tasse *n* cup
taub *adj* deaf
die Tauchausrüstung diving equipment
tauchen *v* dive
das Taxi taxi
das Team team
der Teelöffel teaspoon
der Teich pond
das Teil part (for car)
das Telefon *n* phone
das schnurlose Telefon wireless phone
der Telefonanruf phone call
die Telefonkarte phone card
die Telefonnummer phone number
der Teller plate

der Tempel temple (religious)
das Tennis tennis
der Termin appointment
der Terminal terminal (airport)
teuer expensive
der Text *n* text
das Theater theater
tief deep
die Tiefkühlkost frozen food
das Tier animal
der Tisch table
die Toilette restroom [toilet BE]
das Toilettenpapier
  toilet paper
der Topf *n* pot
die Töpferwaren pottery (pots)
die Tour *n* tour
der Tourist tourist
traditionell traditional
traurig sad
treffen meet
das Treffen meeting
trennen disconnect (computer)
die Treppe stairs
trinken *v* drink
das Trinkwasser drinking water
der Tropfen *n* drop (medicine)
das T-Shirt T-shirt
die Tür door
der Turm tower
die Turnschuhe sneaker

U

die U-Bahn subway [underground
  BE]
die U-Bahn-Haltestelle subway
  [underground BE] station
über *prep* over;
  ~ **Nacht** overnight;
  ~**fallen** *v* mug
die Übergröße plus size
überhitzen overheat (car)
übersetzen translate
überweisen *v* transfer (money)
um (die Ecke) around (the corner)
umändern alter
umarmen *v* hug
die Umkleidekabine fitting room
der Umschlag envelope
umsteigen *v* change (buses); ~
  v transfer (change trains/flights)
umtauschen *v* exchange (money)
umwerfend stunning
unbeaufsichtigt unattended
der Unfall accident
die Universität university
die Unterhaltung entertainment
  (amusement)
die Unterhose underwear
  [underpants BE]
die Unterkunft accommodation
die Unterlegplane groundcloth
unterschreiben *v* sign

der Untertitel *n* subtitle
die Unterwäsche underwear
der Urin urine
der Urlaub vacation [BE holiday]

V

die Vagina vagina
vaginal vaginal; **die ~e Entzündung** vaginal infection
der Vater father
der V-Ausschnitt V-neck
der Veganer *n* vegan
der Vegetarier *n* vegetarian
der Ventilator fan (appliance)
verbieten *v* prohibit
verbinden *v* connect (internet)
die Verbindung connection
die Vereinigten Staaten United States (U.S.)
verfügbar available
vergewaltigen *v* rape
die Vergewaltigung *n* rape
der Vergnügungspark amusement park
verheiratet married
verkaufen *v* sell
verlangen *v* charge (cost)
verlieren *v* lose (something)
verlobt engaged
verloren lost
verschlucken *v* swallow

verschneit snowy
verschreiben *v* prescribe (medication)
versenden *v* ship
die Versicherung insurance
die Versicherungsgesellschaft insurance company
die Versicherungskarte insurance card
die Verstauchung *n* sprain
verstehen understand
die Verstopfung constipation
verwitwet widowed
verzögern *v* delay
viel much; **~** a lot; **~en Dank** thank you; **wie ~** how much
violett *adj* purple
die Visitenkarte business card
das Visum visa
das Vitamin vitamin
die Vitrine display case
der Vogel bird
die Volksmusik folk music
das Volleyballspiel volleyball game
Vollzeit- full-time
vor before; **Viertel ~ vier** a quarter to four
die Vorfahrt right of way
die Vorhersage *n* forecast
die Vorspeise appetizer [starter BE]

vorstellen *v* introduce (person)
vorübergehend temporary

W

wählen *v* dial
während during
die Währung currency
der Währungsumtausch currency exchange
der Wald forest
die Wanderroute walking route
die Wanderschuhe hiking boots
die Wanduhr wall clock
wann when (time)
die Ware *n* good; ~ product
die Waren goods
warm *adj* warm (temperature)
warten wait
der Warteraum waiting room
die Wartezeit *n* waiting period
was what
das Waschbecken *n* sink
die Wäscherei laundry (facility)
der Wäscheservice laundry service
die Waschmaschine washing machine
waschmaschinenfest machine washable
das Waschmittel detergent
der Waschsalon laundromat [launderette BE]

der Wasserfall waterfall
die Wasserski water skis
das Wechselgeld *n* change (money)
der Wechselkurs exchange rate
wechseln *v* change
die Wechselstube currency exchange office
wecken *v* wake
der Weckruf wake-up call
weich soft
das Weingut vineyard
die Weinkarte wine list
weiß *adj* white
das Weißgold white gold
weit *adv* far (distance); ~ *adj* loose (fit)
weitsichtig far [long BE]- sighted
das Wellness-Center spa
wenig *adj* little (not much)
weniger less
wer who
der Wert value
wertvoll valuable
der Westen *n* west
das Wetter weather
wickeln *v* change (baby)
wie how; ~ **viel** how much
wiederholen repeat
willkommen *adj* welcome
die Windel diaper [nappy BE]

die Wirbelsäule spine (body part)
wireless wireless
wo where
die Woche week
das Wochenende weekend
wöchentlich weekly
der Wohnwagen mobile home
die Wolle wool
wunder schön beautiful
die Wüste *n* desert

---

der Zahn tooth
der Zahnarzt dentist
die Zahnpaste toothpaste
der Zeh *n* toe
der Zehennagel toenail
das Zeichen symbol (keyboard)
zeigen *v* show (somebody something)
die Zeit time
der Zeitraum period (of time)
die Zeitung newspaper

der Zeitungskiosk newsstand
das Zelt tent
der Zelthering tent peg
die Zeltstange tent pole
der Zentimeter centimeter
zerbrochen broken (smashed)
das Zertifikat certificate
ziehen *v* extract (tooth);
 ~ *v* pull (door sign)
die Zigarette cigarette
die Zigarre cigar
das Zimmer room
der Zimmerschlüssel room key
der Zimmerservice room service
das Zinn pewter
der Zoll customs; ~ duty (tax)
zollfrei duty-free
der Zoo zoo
zu *adv* too; ~ *prep* to
der Zug train
die Zunge tongue
zurückgeben *v* return (something)
der Zutritt *n* access

Berlitz®

speaking your language

phrase book & dictionary
phrase book & CD

Available in: Arabic, Cantonese Chinese, Croatian, Czech, Danish, Dutch, English*, Finnish*, French, German, Greek, Hebrew*, Hindi, Hungarian*, Indonesian, Italian, Japanese, Korean, Latin American Spanish, Mandarin Chinese, Mexican Spanish, Norwegian, Polish, Portuguese, Romanian*, Russian, Spanish, Swedish, Thai, Turkish, Vietnamese

*Book only